HISTORIC KIRKINTILLOCH

HISTORIC
KIRKINTILLOCH

Archaeology and development

Martin Rorke, E Patricia Dennison, Simon Stronach
and Russel Coleman

THE SCOTTISH BURGH SURVEY

sustainable thriving achieving
East Dunbartonshire Council
www.eastdunbarton.gov.uk

Published by the Council for British Archaeology and Historic Scotland
First published in 2009

Copyright © 2009 Historic Scotland
The moral right of the authors has been asserted.
British Library Cataloguing in Publication Data
A catalogue for this book is available from the British Library

Edited by Catrina Appleby, CBA and Mark Watson, Historic Scotland
Page design and typesetting by Carnegie Publishing Ltd

Printing and binding: Information Press, Oxford
ISBN: 978-1-902771-58-8

Council for British Archaeology
St Mary's House,
66 Bootham,
York YO30 7BZ
www.britarch.ac.uk

Historic Scotland
Longmore House
Salisbury Place
Edinburgh
EH9 1SH
Tel. 0131 668 8600
Fax. 0131 668 8669
www.historic-scotland.gov.uk

Cover: Kirkintilloch from the air, looking east, 1990
(By courtesy of RCAHMS, © Crown copyright RCAHMS)

Insets: The Hudson Fountain, Peel Park
(By courtesy of East Dunbartonshire Information and Archives);
K6 type telephone kiosks, made by the Lion Foundry

Contents

Figures

Colour broadsheet

Abbreviations

APS	*Acts of the Parliaments of Scotland* T Thomson and C Innes (eds) (Edinburgh, 1814–75)
CDS	*Calendar of Documents Relating to Scotland* J Bain *et al* (eds) (Edinburgh, 1881–1986)
DES	*Discovery and Excavation in Scotland*
EDA	East Dunbartonshire Information and Archives, Kirkintilloch
Glas Recs	*Extracts from the Records of the Burgh of Glasgow* J D Marwick *et al* (eds) (Scottish Burgh Records Society, 1876–1916)
GUARD	Glasgow University Archaeological Research Division
Horne, *Kirkintilloch*	*Kirkintilloch* J Horne (ed) (Kirkintilloch, 1910, reprinted 1993)
Kirk Ct Bk	*The Court Book of the Burgh of Kirkintilloch 1658–1694* G S Pryde (ed) (SHS, 1963)
NAS	National Archives of Scotland
NLS	National Library of Scotland
NMRS	National Monuments Record of Scotland.
NSA	*The New Statistical Account of Scotland* (Edinburgh, 1845)
OSA	*The Statistical Account of Scotland, 1791–99* J Sinclair (ed) New edition I R Grant and D J Withrington (eds) (Wakefield, 1978)
Proc Soc Antiq Scot	*Proceedings of the Society of Antiquaries of Scotland*
RCAHMS	Royal Commission on the Ancient and Historical Monuments of Scotland
RCRB	*Extracts from the Records of the Convention of Royal Burghs of Scotland* J D Marwick (ed) (Edinburgh, 1870–1918)
RMS	*Register of the Great Seal of Scotland* J M Thomson *et al* (eds) (Edinburgh, 1882–1914)
RPC	*Register of the Privy Council of Scotland* J H Burton *et al* (eds) First series (Edinburgh, 1877–98), second series (Edinburgh, 1899–1908), third series (Edinburgh, 1908–70)
RRS	*Regesta Regum Scottorum* G W S Barrow *et al* (eds) (Edinburgh, 1960–)
RSS	*Register of the Privy Seal of Scotland* M Livingstone *et al* (eds) (Edinburgh, 1908–)
SBRS	Scottish Burgh Records Society
SHS	Scottish History Society
SRS	Scottish Record Society

Scots Peerage	*The Scots Peerage* J Balfour Paul (ed) (Edinburgh, 1904–14)
SDLM	Strathkelvin District Libraries and Museums
SUAT	Scottish Urban Archaeological Trust Ltd
TA	*Accounts of the Lord High Treasurer of Scotland* T Dickson *et al* (eds) (Edinburgh, 1877–)

Acknowledgements

The authors wish to thank Don Martin, Assistant Manager of Information and Archives of the East Dunbartonshire Information and Archives at William Patrick Library, for his painstaking comments and assistance with an early draft of this Survey. Catriona Macdonald, Partnership Planner, East Dunbartonshire Council, also gave helpful comments on the Survey. Valuable assistance was also provided by Sarah Chubb, Archivist and Records Officer of the East Dunbartonshire Information and Archives, Peter McCormack, Curator of the Auld Kirk Museum, Hugh McBrien of the West of Scotland Archaeological Service, David Swan of the Glasgow University Archaeological Research Division, David Perry of SUAT Ltd and Morag Cross in Kirkintilloch.

We are grateful to the staff of the Royal Commission on the Ancient and Historical Monuments of Scotland, the National Archives of Scotland and the National Library of Scotland (George IV Bridge and Causewayside).

We also wish to thank Dr Margaret Munro for her research into Kirkintilloch conducted for the Survey and Duncan McAra for proof reading. David Breeze checked the text in particular regarding the Antonine Wall, Mark Watson made a contribution on hand loom shops and edits were also made by Martin Brann and Dawn McDowell, all of Historic Scotland.

Research for this Survey was conducted in the winter of 2003/04. Mapping was by Caroline Normann and Mike Middleton of Headland Archaeology Ltd.

1 Use of the Burgh Survey

Continual evolution is the essence of urban life. Change is inevitable in towns and is what gives them their vitality. Yet it is the imprint of history that gives localities their distinctive character. Conservation is a matter of ensuring that the qualities that define a place are maintained while change continues to happen. Managing change requires an understanding of that character.

The Scottish Burgh Survey is a guide to the archaeological resource in towns, published by the Council for British Archaeology on behalf of Historic Scotland. It helps to influence decision-makers and to set the research agenda on questions that may be answered by archaeology where development occurs. Publications in the latest series are at http://www.britarch.ac.uk/pubs/latest.html.

This third series of Burgh Surveys is intended to furnish local authorities, developers and residents with reliable information to help manage the archaeology and historic environment of Scotland's urban centres. It offers comprehensive and consistent base-line information against which research, regeneration, and land-use planning objectives may be set. It also guides the general reader in researching the rich history and archaeology of Scotland's historic burghs.

In its role as a tool for local authorities to use in the planning process, the first point of reference in this volume is the colour-coded town plan (**fig 28** and broadsheet), which depicts areas of prime archaeological interest. It is often the case, however, that discoveries are made outwith those areas, which will necessitate a reassessment of our state of knowledge of the burgh of Kirkintilloch.

In 2008 two significant changes were made to designations:
- UNESCO inscribed the Antonine Wall as an extension to the Frontiers of the Roman Empire World Heritage Site. Its area is shown in dark green on the broadsheet and **fig 28**.
- Peel Park Conservation Area was enlarged by East Dunbartonshire Council following a character appraisal and has been renamed Kirkintilloch Conservation Area. Details may be obtained from the Local Authority.

Further research into the archaeological potential of a site within the historic town can be gleaned from local and national libraries and archives. The PASTMAP website (http://www.PASTMAP.org.uk) can also be consulted. This interactive website, supported jointly by Historic Scotland and the Royal Commission on the Ancient and Historical Monuments of Scotland, allows anyone with internet access to search data on Scotland's historic environment including the sites protected by statute, scheduled ancient monuments, and listed buildings.

Both this Burgh Survey and the PASTMAP website provide information only. Where development is being considered advice should be sought in all cases directly from East Dunbartonshire Council, Partnership and Planning, The Triangle, Kirkintilloch Road, Bishopbriggs, Glasgow, G64 2TR.

A note about names

The town of Dumbarton retains that name, but the county name changed to Dunbartonshire soon after the Act of Parliament in 1889 which established Dumbartonshire County Council [sic]. The county clerk persuaded the Ordnance Survey to adopt the new name in the 1930s, and the Post Office and newspapers followed suit in the 1960s.[1] This book uses the name as cited in the source, and so most historic references refer to Dumbartonshire. The local authority is East Dunbartonshire Council.

The place name Inchbelly now lives on as Inchbelle Farm, but 'Inchbelly Bridge' is used here.

The Old Aisle or Auld Isle, or on the 1st Edition OS map Old Ayle, has had various permutations, and here again the name as it appears in the source is used.

Notes

1   I M MacPhail, Dumbarton Castle (1979), 202–3

2 Site and setting

Introduction

The medieval settlement of Kirkintilloch is now surrounded by modern suburbs to the west, east and south (**figs 1 & 2**). The historic core of the town occupies a hill overlooking the valley of the Kelvin to the north and that of the Luggie Water to the east (**fig 1**). Although the surrounding landscape has been much changed, it remains possible to appreciate the strategic importance of this location, especially its command over the lower-lying areas between the town and the imposing Campsie Fells to the north (**fig 1**). The town's name reflects this, originating as 'Caerpentaloch', being two parts Brythonic and one part Gaelic, later developing into the Brythonic Gaelic *caer* (fort) - *ceann* (head) - *tulaich* (hillock).[1]

Although the presence of the Campsie Fells lends the impression that Kirkintilloch occupies the edge of a valley stretching across the central belt of Scotland, it is actually located centrally in the great Midland Valley, which stretches from Stonehaven to Greenock in the north, and from Dunbar to Girvan in the south.[2] The Campsie Fells would have formed a barrier to traffic travelling from Glasgow to the north-east[3] and hence the town not only lies on one of the routes between Edinburgh and Glasgow but also on one that led to the important medieval centre of Stirling.

Land use and geology

The Campsie Fells are formed from basalt lavas that were the product of volcanic activity in the Carboniferous period (350 to 270 million years ago).[4] At this time the area was covered with tropical forests, and gradually these led to the formation of the coal seams that have had a profound impact on the development of the town. The underlying bedrock is comprised mainly of sedimentary sandstone, which has been quarried nearby at Bishopbriggs and Dullatur, the latter providing the stone for the Town Hall.[5]

The agricultural potential of the land around the town is somewhat limited by a tendency to contain poorly draining clayey soils in this area of high rainfall, and hence pastoral farming was traditionally favoured by the region's inhabitants.[6] However, the arable potential can still be classed as good where drainage is not a problem.[7] The uplands of the Campsie Fells with their rough grazing were suitable for sheep farming.[8]

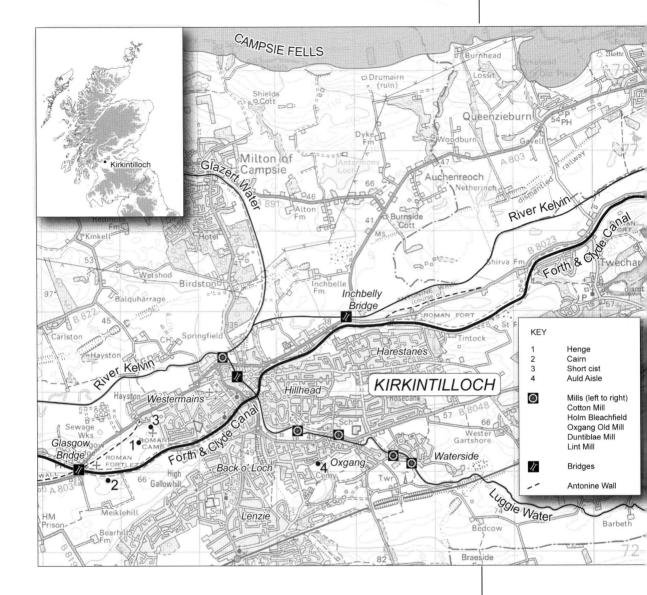

FIGURE 1:
Location map: Kirkintilloch
and surrounding area

Economy

It is hard to imagine today, but for most of its history Kirkintilloch was a small, rural centre and market town, with associated service industries such as inns and tailoring. Like many of the so-called hillfoot villages the traditional mainstay of the local economy was the production of textiles, especially processing the wool produced by sheep reared on the nearby uplands.[9] The transformation of the economy can be traced to the opening of the Forth & Clyde Canal (**fig 1**) between Grangemouth and Kirkintilloch in 1773 when the Hillhead basin became Scotland's first inland port.[10] This made the town a trading hub, and cotton-spinning quickly became a principal activity.[11] The movement of coal through the town via the Monkland and

Kirkintilloch Railway, which opened in 1826, was also important. Other industries which grew up in this period were shipyards and iron foundries.[12] During the twentieth century competition from rail and road meant the canal lost its importance and the general decline in heavy manufacturing industries throughout Scotland affected Kirkintilloch along with many other towns. However, by the 1980s there was a large enough concentration of multinational electronic firms in the central belt to earn it the nickname 'Silicon Glen'. The close proximity of Glasgow and good communications with the surrounding area meant the people of Kirkintilloch were well placed to take advantage of this revival.

FIGURE 2:
Aerial view of Kirkintilloch, 1990 (By courtesy of RCAHMS; © Crown copyright RCAHMS)

Sources of information

The once obvious nature of the town's Roman antiquities meant that Kirkintilloch attracted antiquarian interest from the eighteenth century and its visible remains are described with notes and drawings.[13] Archaeological excavations within Peel Park (**fig 29.1**) to investigate the Roman remains were first undertaken at the end of the nineteenth century, and there are currently three published articles describing what has been found, the latest of these neatly summarising the information available at the end of the twentieth century.[14] More recently, some archaeological work was undertaken alongside landscaping within the Park during 2002.[15] Excavations within the burgh, concentrating on the town's medieval remains, were undertaken in the 1970s. Information relating to these projects is stored in the East Dunbartonshire Information and Archives within the William Patrick Library (**fig 29.2**) and by the Museum Service in the Auld Kirk Museum (**fig 29.3**). The archive of an excavation undertaken in the 1980s is currently held by SUAT Ltd, Perth.

Historic maps of the town, starting with the first detailed map made by William Roy from 1747 to 1755 (see **fig 4**), are a good source of information concerning the town's development. The first edition Ordnance Survey town plan made in 1859 is available online through the National Library of Scotland digital maps service (http://www.nls.uk/digitallibrary/index.html).

RCAHMS holds information relating to chance finds in and around the town, accessible through its Canmore database, which can be accessed through the internet (http://www.rcahms.gov.uk/search.html). It also holds a collection of historic photographs and pictures relating to the town. Many more historic photographs are readily available at the William Patrick Library.

The Pastmap internet site (http://www.rcahms.gov.uk/search.html), run jointly by Historic Scotland and the Royal Commission on the Ancient and Historical Monuments of Scotland, contains information relating to the town's listed buildings and scheduled ancient monuments.

There is a significant body of secondary source material that examines the history of Kirkintilloch (see Bibliography). The work of Don Martin is particularly noteworthy. There are also numerous manuscript and printed sources, at both local and national levels. Especially important for the pre-1800 period is the printed *Court Book of the Burgh of Kirkintilloch 1658–1694*, which offers an excellent insight into the topography of the burgh and the workings of the community. Valuable information is also contained in manuscripts housed in the East Dunbartonshire Archives, for instance the Burgh Court Book 1729–98, the Treasurer Receipt Books 1615–1772, and the Papers found in Westermains, Kirkintilloch. However, due to time constraints, thorough investigation into these manuscript sources was not possible. The National Archives of Scotland contain material which has not been consulted, but which could advance our understanding of Kirkintilloch in the seventeenth and eighteenth centuries; this includes Kirk Session records, the 1690 Hearth Tax, and evidence from sasines and testaments.

The range of documentary sources available for studies into Kirkintilloch in the nineteenth and twentieth centuries is extensive. Town council records and accounts; valuation rolls; burgess papers; records on buildings, roads and amenities; materials relating to businesses, and private papers are all available in the East Dunbartonshire Archives. There are also newspapers, contemporary accounts, and numerous photographs relating to Kirkintilloch from the mid- to late nineteenth century. The limitations of time meant that examination of this material was no more than cursory, although many of these sources have been consulted by other authors, whose works appear in the Bibliography.

Listed buildings and scheduled ancient monuments

Peel Park and the Forth and Clyde Canal are scheduled ancient monuments (**fig 29.1** & **29.4**). These areas, and their setting within the wider landscape, have been given statutory protection. The Antonine Wall (indicated in dark green on **fig 28**) is also part of the Frontiers of the Roman Empire World Heritage Site. The archaeological remains of the Wall that lie within Peel Park are scheduled but this area does not extend beneath the town. In addition, the Roman temporary camp at Westermains, to the west, and Auchendavy Roman fort, to the east (north of Harestanes), are also scheduled ancient monuments (**fig 1**).[16]

Twenty-six buildings or structures within the central area of the town are listed by the Scottish Ministers as buildings of special architectural or historic interest. The list is maintained by Historic Scotland. Buildings are assigned to one of three categories according to their relative importance. Protection applies equally to the interior and exterior of all listed buildings regardless of category. Listed buildings can include anything from medieval churches to phone boxes. Two structures in Kirkintilloch are Category A-listed and thus considered to be of national or international importance. This status can be derived from historic or architectural interest, or a combination of the two. In Kirkintilloch the Auld Kirk (**fig 29.3**) and the Luggie Water Aqueduct (**fig 29.5**) are listed Category A. Seventeen structures are listed at Category B, or of regional importance. There are three concentrations of these, one on High Street to the north of The Cross, the Westermains farm buildings on West High Street, and a group of buildings in Eastside. These three concentrations represent the areas with the best survival of post-medieval vernacular buildings in the town. Seven buildings are listed at Category C(S), or of local importance.

Archaeology of the area before the town developed

Prehistory

When the first settlers arrived in Scotland following the end of the last Ice Age around 10,000 years ago, the landscape would have been heavily wooded and travel would have been easiest along river valleys.[17] It is likely that the area around the Kelvin valley and its tributaries would have been settled from an early date. In the early prehistoric period people lived by hunting and gathering in a land shared with deer, elk, aurochs, bear and boar.[18] From around 4000 BC domesticated plants and animals were introduced, farming took hold and the land was cleared.[19]

No remains or chance finds dating from this early period have been recovered from the Kirkintilloch area, although undoubtedly it was settled. What is likely to be the earliest known surviving site is a small henge monument visible as a cropmark to the west of the town (**fig 1**).[20] Henges were circular enclosures formed by cutting a ditch and placing the upcast material on the outside. Archaeological excavations elsewhere have suggested that they were religious or sacred places built in the later Neolithic period, that is from around 3000 BC. Often they contained timber or stone circles and the latter seems to be the case with this example. On present evidence, henge sites are very rare in the west of Scotland.[21]

An urn containing a human cremation, perhaps from beneath a cairn, and an empty short cist, each probably of Bronze Age date, were discovered to the west of the town in the 1920s (**fig 1**).[22] It seems likely that the settlements associated with these burials were located in the immediate vicinity. Further evidence for Bronze Age settlement was discovered during excavations for a sewer near Inchbelle Farm to the north of the town (**fig 1**).[23] Several pits containing charcoal and pottery were recorded and these may be the only remains left after years of ploughing over a much more substantial settlement. No Iron Age remains have been identified in the vicinity and the beginnings of tangible settlement at Kirkintilloch, and probably the origin of the place name itself, must be traced to a foreign invader, namely the Romans.

The Roman period

When referring to this part of Scotland the Romans described it as being occupied by a tribe called the *Damnonii*.[24] The area was first occupied during the military incursions of the governor Agricola who built bases across the Forth/Clyde isthmus around AD 80.[25] Little is known about these and it was not until AD 142 under the rule of the Emperor Antoninus Pius that the famous Wall was built. The presumed course of the Wall is shown in **figs 1** and **29.6**. It was built from turfs placed on a stone base and is thought to have reached a height of some 3m, possibly crowned with a timber breastwork for additional protection.[26] To the front of the Wall was a wide and deep ditch. It would seem that the Wall was defended by forts placed every 2 miles (3km) or so, with fortlets, it would appear, at every mile in between. It is thought that beacon platforms were placed at strategic points to maintain communication north and south.[27] The Wall was constructed by three legions which commemorated their work with carved stones called 'distance slabs'. Two of these found in the vicinity of Kirkintilloch can be seen in the Hunterian Museum, at the University of Glasgow, and a cast of one is in the Auld Kirk Museum.

As it crossed the area later occupied by the town, the Wall was constructed strategically along a ridge overlooking low ground to the north. A fort was constructed at Kirkintilloch because it lies on a rise on this ridge, with command over the crossing point of the Luggie Water to the east. The forts on the Wall were routinely manned by auxiliaries though legionaries were sometimes used. The principal buildings were a headquarters building, a commander's house, granaries, barracks and a bath-house.[28] Many of the forts had annexes, while civil settlements probably existed outside most forts.[29] It is known that extensive field systems existed at some forts, and recent excavations have suggested that these may even have stretched to the north of the Wall.[30] The forts were connected by the so-called 'Military Way', a road which ran on the south side of the Wall. The Wall and forts were all abandoned sometime around AD 160.

The Dark Ages

In all probability the place name Kirkintilloch refers to the Roman fort. The name, however, is part Brythonic and part Gaelic rather than derived from Latin. Following the Romans' departure, the name would have been preserved not by written documents but in the spoken language of the area's inhabitants. Unfortunately, the lack of written documents, which is how the so-called 'Dark Ages' came by its name, means very little is known about the area from the departure of the Romans until the founding of the medieval burgh. On a general level we know that Roman roads frequently continued to be used and forts were reused; it is not known if this was the case at Kirkintilloch, but it is certainly a possibility. From the seventh to the ninth century the area lay somewhere in the middle of the ill-defined territories held, and frequently fought over, by the Scots of Argyll, the Angles of Northumbria and the Picts.[31] By the tenth century the Picts and Scots had formed an alliance that was the genesis of the Scottish nation. A tenuous link to this period survives in the dedication of the old parish church of the Auld Aisle to St Ninian (**fig 1**). Ninian was the earliest Christian missionary in Scotland, associated with a monastic community in Whithorn, Dumfries and Galloway;[32] although little is known about his life, he is thought to have converted the southern Picts. Many dedications to Ninian are recorded and their frequent occurrence near Roman roads has been taken to indicate that these were being used during his missionary work.

The town today

Development in the nineteenth and twentieth centuries has greatly increased the area covered by the town (**fig 1**). To the east Hillhead and Harestanes, to the south Oxgang and Lenzie, and to the west Westermains, have all spread far beyond the town's medieval and post-medieval limits. The northern edge has not seen the same dramatic expansion due to the steep slope with lower, wetter ground at its base. For the purposes of this study the limits of the historic town are defined as Glasgow Road in the north, Eastside in the east, Townhead in the south and Peel Park in the west. Discussion of the town's archaeology has been divided into three areas, shown in **fig 29**: Area 1 containing the town's Roman and medieval fortifications; Area 2 the medieval town; and Area 3 post-medieval expansion to the eighteenth century. These three areas will be discussed after a general account of the town's historic past and significance.

Notes

1   M Darton, *The Dictionary of Place Names in Scotland* (Orpington, 1994), 164; RCAHMS, *Stirlingshire* (Edinburgh, 1963), i, 6

2   I B Cameron and D Stephenson, *The Midland Valley of Scotland* (London, 1985), 1

3   *ibid*

4   J Gifford and F A Walker, *The Buildings of Scotland: Stirling and Central Scotland* (London, 2002), 3

5   *ibid*, 3–7

6   *ibid*, 2

7   J T Coppock, *An Agricultural Atlas of Scotland* (Edinburgh, 1976), figs 3–6

8   *ibid*, fig 47

9   Gifford and Walker, *Buildings of Scotland*, 98

10 J R Hume, *The Industrial Archaeology of Scotland 1. The Lowlands and Borders* (London, 1976), 106

11 Gifford and Walker, *Buildings of Scotland*, 565

12 Hume, *Industrial Archaeology*, 106–11

13 J Horsley, *Britannia Romana of the Roman Antiquities of Britain* (London, 1732); W Roy, *The Military Antiquities of the Romans in Northern Britain* (London, 1793)

14 G Macdonald, 'Further discoveries on the line of the Antonine Wall', *Proc Soc Antiq Scot*, lix (1924–25), 290–5; A S Robertson, 'Miscellanea Romano-Caledonica', *Proc Soc Antiq Scot*, xcvii (1963–64), 180–8; L J F Keppie, G B Bailey, A J Dunwell, J H McBrien and K Speller, 'Some excavations on the line of the Antonine Wall 1985–93', *Proc Soc Antiq Scot*, cxxv (1995), 650–68

15 D Swan and H James, Peel Park, Kirkintilloch (unpublished GUARD client report, 2003)

16 NMRS, *NS67SW 24; NS67SE 12 & 42*

17 J N Graham Ritchie, 'Prehistoric and Early Historic Stirling and Central Scotland', in Gifford and Walker, *Buildings of Scotland*, 9–11

18 B Finlayson and K J Edwards, 'The Mesolithic', in K J Edwards and I B M Ralston (eds), *Scotland after the Ice Age* (Edinburgh, 1997), 113

19 G Barclay, *Farmers, Temples and Tombs: Scotland in the Neolithic and Early Bronze Age* (Edinburgh, 1998), 12–13

20 RCHAMS, *NS67SW 27*

21 G J Barclay, 'The Neolithic', in Edwards and Ralston (eds), *Scotland after the Ice Age*, fig 8.2

22 RCHAMS, *NS67SW 8*; J Fletcher 'Two Kirkintilloch antiquities: carved dragon head and short cist', *Proc Soc Antiq Scot*, lxxxvi (1951–52), 202

23 P Masser and A MacSween, 'Early Bronze Age Pits at Inchbelle Farm, Kirkintilloch, East Dunbartonshire', *Scottish Archaeological Journal*, xxiv, part i (2002), 49–60

24 J N Graham Ritchie, 'Prehistoric and Early Historic Stirling and Central Scotland', 11

25 D J Breeze, 'The Romans in Stirling and Central Scotland', in Gifford and Walker, *Buildings of Scotland*, 12; D J Breeze, *Roman Scotland* (1996)

26 *ibid*, 13

27 *ibid*, 13

28 *ibid*, 13–14

29 *ibid*, 15

30 A H Blair and M Hastie, Kelvin Valley Sewer Stage 2 Phase 1 Archaeological Data Structure Report (unpublished Headland Archaeology client report, 2000)

31 I Fisher, 'The Early Christian Period in Stirling and Central Scotland', in Gifford and Walker, *Buildings of Scotland*, 15–17

32 P Hill, *Whithorn and St Ninian: the Excavation of a Monastic Town 1984–91* (Stroud, 1997)

3 History and archaeology

Roman period and later prehistory

If, as appears likely, there was a pre-Roman settlement around Kirkintilloch, it has left little surviving evidence except for the graves discovered in local sandpits.[1] There was, however, definitely settlement at Kirkintilloch in the Roman period. Roman bronze coins from the first century have been unearthed, suggesting that Kirkintilloch may have been the site of an Agricolan fort (AD 77–84), although they may have been imported later during the construction and occupation of the Antonine Wall.[2] The entire line of the Wall at Kirkintilloch has not been conclusively established. Between Auchendavy and the centre of Kirkintilloch, the rampart and ditch are hardly visible, but excavations have established its line south of the canal and north of Hillhead Road at Cleddans.[3] It is likely to have passed to the north or under the Auld Kirk, rather than to the south as shown in **figure 29**, along the brow of the hill towards the remains found in the north-west corner of Peel Park (**fig 29.1**). Excavations there revealed that the ditch was at least 10.5m wide and the stone base of the rampart about 4.5m wide. A drain or culvert was also constructed at the time the base was laid.[4]

The fort is represented on the arms of the burgh and the burgh seal. Early antiquarians assumed the grassy mound and ditch towards the north of the Peel were its remains, but in fact this was the site of the medieval castle.[5] Recent excavations have shown that the fort extended as far south as Union Street, and suggest that the internal area was about 1.4ha, rather larger than most Antonine forts. A further ditch running parallel to the southern defences may have been an additional defence or may have served to enclose a small annexe. The basal fills of the ditches have been found to be waterlogged as can be seen in **figure 23**. Waterlogging is beneficial to the archaeological resource as rare organic materials such as wood and leather may be preserved; in this case Roman sandals were recovered. The fort must have occupied a very strong position, sited on top of a long ridge which descended gently to the east and more steeply on the west, with a sharp drop on the north. Inside the fort the remains of streets, gutters, hearths and rows of post-holes belonging to narrow wooden buildings have been discovered.[6] It should be pointed out, however, that the excavations generally involved only small trenches and the fort's layout remains poorly understood. Some indirect evidence has been interpreted as suggesting that there may have been an annexe possibly containing a bath-house to the south and east of the fort. Antonine artefacts found in the vicinity include Roman building stones, a quernstone, a clay jar, coins, spearheads, fragments of tiles, pottery, bones, glass and shoe-leather.[7] Stray Roman coins have been found from the period after the Wall was abandoned in about AD 163; these could indicate either a protracted withdrawal period or continued Roman patrols in the area.[8]

Little is known about Kirkintilloch in the centuries immediately after the Roman army withdrew. Early historians speculated that it was the site of the battle of Chirchind at the end of the sixth century,[9] when the king of Dalriada's three sons were killed, but this identification is now not given much credence.[10] The name Kirkintilloch in its earliest written form 'Caerpentaloch', 'fort at the head of the ridge', is at least as old as the tenth century.[11]

The Middle Ages and the sixteenth century

On 2 October 1211, William I (1165–1214) granted to William Comyn the liberty of a burgh at Kirkintilloch.[12] As a burgh of barony, only the second to be created in Scotland, its rights and privileges were less significant than those of a royal burgh, but its right to hold a market on Thursday must have been important. There was clearly a significant settlement in existence by the early thirteenth century. The early township may have been situated at Peel Brae, in close proximity to the castle at the Peel, a situation which would have offered both protection and opportunities through supplying the garrison with goods and services.

Surprisingly little is known about the castle. It was built in the twelfth or very early thirteenth century, almost certainly by the Comyns, a Norman family whose lands were originally in southern Scotland. By the second half of the twelfth century, their estates also included the barony of Lenzie, which extended from Kirkintilloch to Cumbernauld. Little now remains of the castle, but it seems to have been a relatively early stone castle surrounded by a square ditched enclosure (*see* pp 58–9 and **fig 22**). The Roman ditch may have been utilised for the northern portion, and the eastern part was 5.5m deep.[13] The remains were greatly reduced in the 1830s when the western part was levelled to form a kaleyard, and about this time much of the ditch was filled in.[14] A drawbridge over the eastern ditch gave access to the castle yard. Some of the stones used for the castle came from the old Roman fort. Horsley described the remains in 1732 as having a 'double rampart of hewn stone, strongly cemented with lime'.[15] During excavations in 1899 parts of the stone foundations of the north, south and west walls were exposed; in places the walls were over 3m thick.[16] The castle was supplied with water from two wells with stone-built shafts, one on the north-west of the courtyard and the other on the west face of the mound.[17] Further east, at Peel Brae, stood the Blue Tower (**fig 3**), which is believed to have been an outpost of the castle; it survived in a dilapidated state until the nineteenth century.[18] A group of 'several slender pillars with

FIGURE 3:
Peel Brae, looking south,
c 1820; the partially
demolished building
may be the 'Blue Tower'
(By courtesy of East
Dunbartonshire Information
and Archives)

ornamented capitals … were dug up within the ruins and adjoining field'.[19] Enthusiasts for the Roman period considered they might have been the remains of a 'small temple', but they were later dated to around 1200,[20] and may indicate some form of chapel associated with the castle.

A church dedicated to St Ninian was established in the barony around the middle of the twelfth century at the 'Auld Aisle', Oxgang (**fig 1**). It was erected near the ford over the Luggie, about a mile south-east of the castle and any settlement around it.[21] As the parish church it served the old parish of Lenzie which covered from Kirkintilloch to Cumbernauld, and the siting must therefore have been significant.[22] The founder was, in the past, believed to have been Thorold Comyn, proprietor of the barony of Kirkintilloch and Cumbernauld in c 1140, and there has been speculation that it was built on an ancient Ninian foundation. The association of Thorold Comyn with the foundation of the church is, however, now thought to be incorrect and there is no clear evidence that it was founded as early as 1140.[23] At the end of the twelfth century William, son of Thorold, sheriff of Stirling, granted the church of Kirkintilloch, together with half a carucate (or ploughgate) of land, to Cambuskenneth Abbey, and this gift was confirmed by Pope Celestine III in 1195.[24] There were further confirmations in the thirteenth century, including a charter from Alexander II (1214–49) in 1226, which restated the grant of the church of Kirkintilloch to Cambuskenneth Abbey, together with an oxgate of land which adjoined the church land on the east side.[25] In the late thirteenth century another charter by John Comyn confirmed the oxgate and added 'the whole land adjoining that oxgate, between Luggy and Buthlane, cultivated and uncultivated, as far as the said oxgate of land extends, with one acre of land on the east side of the said oxgate'.[26] In addition, the canons of Cambuskenneth Abbey were to receive 30 loads of peat from the peat-moss at Kirkintilloch annually 'at the sight of the bailies of Kirkintilloch' – the first mention of a bailie in the burgh. In 1275 the papal assessment (one-tenth of all ecclesiastic revenues) shows that the vicar of Kirkintilloch was taxed at £2 13s 4d, suggesting annual revenue was £26 13s 4d.[27]

In 1451, Sir Robert Fleming of Biggar founded a chaplainry in the parish church of St Ninian, endowing it with annual rents, a tenement and garden in the town of Kirkintilloch.[28] Almost a century later, in 1545, after Malcolm, Lord Fleming, erected a church under a joint parsonage in his barony of Biggar, the church at Kirkintilloch became a collegiate church.[29] At the time of the Reformation the value of the parish church to the monks of Cambuskenneth Abbey was £80.[30] After the Reformation, John, Earl of Mar, acquired the property of Cambuskeneth Abbey, and sold or transferred Kirkintilloch tithes and church to the Earl of Wigtown.[31] It continued to serve as the parish church until the 1640s, when it was demolished and a new church was built in Kirkintilloch. Little now remains of the old church. The Old Belfry at the Auld Aisle (Category A-listed) may have been part of St Ninian's church,[32] but is more likely to have been built in the seventeenth century with the stones from St Ninian's church after it was demolished.[33]

During the Wars of Independence the castle at Kirkintilloch was evidently a stronghold of considerable importance. In the confusion of the wars, prominent Scottish families sometimes fought against the English, and sometimes came to terms with them, but the vicious Bruce-Comyn rivalry was virtually constant. As the Comyns often allied themselves with the English kings, the castle was frequently in English hands. In 1296 they appointed William le Fiz Glay keeper of the castle of Kirkintilloch.[34] In 1300–01 Kirkintilloch Castle again features in English accounts. It was probably taken as the king's army passed en route to Dunipace, and it was then garrisoned by 20 archers, 19 crossbowmen and 27 men at arms.[35] On 1 September 1302 Sir William le Frauncey was appointed to keep the castle of Kirkintilloch until Christmas. He was to command a significant force at the garrison: 28 men at arms and 60 foot soldiers, as well as a chaplain. The castle's defences evidently needed to be strengthened because there is mention of petty officers and various artificers to repair the gate, drawbridge and other defences of the castle. Any necessities were to be secured from the inhabitants of Kirkintilloch at honestly valued prices.[36] The force at Kirkintilloch Castle meant Edward I could order a scouting mission to go by Kirkintilloch on 29 September 1302, 'as near as you can by our enemies'.[37] In the same month three stones for a catapult at Kirkintilloch are recorded.[38] Two years later Sir William's forces at the castle were somewhat depleted in terms of knights and men at arms but he had more crossbowmen and archers.[39] In 1303, however, Sir John Comyn was one of the Scots ambassadors to France, where he was acting in opposition to the interests of the English king. Afterwards he was forced to go to England to make peace with the king, before his forfeited lands in Scotland and England were restored to him.[40] By April 1304 he was again regarded by the English as one of the 'good men in those parts'.[41]

Scottish forces besieged the castle in 1306. It was considered important enough for Robert Wishart, Bishop of Glasgow, to supply timber to make siege engines to be used against the English garrison, timber originally granted to him for a steeple at Glasgow Cathedral.[42] In 1307, however, Kirkintilloch Castle was still in English hands, since it appears in a list of strongholds that Edward I instructed were to be maintained 'to the last extremity against the enemy'.[43] By 1309 Sir Philip de Moubray was constable in charge of Kirkintilloch Castle. A cask of wine is documented as having been sent to him at the castle on 10 September 1309 by Sir Peter Liband, constable of Linlithgow pele.[44] The following year a payment of £54 2s 8d was made for the wages of Sir Philip de Moubray, a knight, 28 esquires and 40 foot soldiers in the garrison at Kirkintilloch Castle between 1 and 27 November.[45] English forces were still resident at the castle in July 1311.[46]

It is not recorded when or how Kirkintilloch Castle fell, but following the triumph of Robert I (1306–29) the power of the Comyns was broken, and it seems probable that like Dalswinton Castle in Galloway, another principal seat of the Comyns, the castle was razed and rendered unusable by the Scots forces. Dismantling conquered strongholds was one of Robert I's fundamental polices.[47] The barony of Lenzie was granted to the Flemings, first to Robert Fleming and, after he died in 1314, to his son Malcolm, who received the 'whole barony of Kirkintilloch with its pertinents which formerly belonged to John Comyn'.[48] Malcolm made Cumbernauld the principal seat of the family. There were no attempts to rebuild the castle and by the start of the fifteenth century charters refer to 'the ground of the old castle of Kirkintilloch'.[49]

Since the burgh had initially been dependent on the Comyns and their presence in the castle, their downfall may have resulted in a decline in the importance of Kirkintilloch, especially as the Flemings chose to establish themselves at Cumbernauld.[50] Indeed, it has been suggested that Kirkintilloch lost its burghal status at the start of the fourteenth century and even ceased to function as a burgh. However, the grant of the barony to Malcolm Fleming by Robert I seems have included the town or burgh, because on 13 May 1373, Robert II (1371–90) confirmed the gift of the *villa* (burgh) of Kirkintilloch by Thomas Fleming to Sir Gilbert Kennedy.[51] Other evidence also points to the continued existence of the burgh:[52] charters in the fifteenth century record annual rents being paid from the burgh and property in the town,[53] while in 1525 and 1528 Malcolm, Lord Fleming, High Chamberlain of Scotland, granted charters to the burgh. These confirmed to the burgesses of Kirkintilloch their ancient rights: 'all and haill the burgh lands and tenements lawfully and by right and custom anciently pertaining to the said burgh of

Kirkintilloch', adding the power to elect bailies, sergeants, officers, writers and clerks of court annually. In return the burgesses were to pay Lord Fleming and his successors twelve merks as feu-duty yearly.[54] These charters are sometimes seen as indicating that Kirkintilloch was re-erected as a burgh of barony, but they could simply indicate a new style of tenure for burghs of barony in which the feu-ferme was accompanied by the participation of burgesses in elections.[55]

The erection of a chapel to the Virgin Mary sometime in the fourteenth century indicates that Kirkintilloch remained a place of some significance. Sir David Fleming granted to the chapel the lands of Drumteblay and a portion of its mill, and this was subsequently confirmed in 1399.[56] In December 1418 Sir William Lyndsay was appointed chaplain of the chaplainry.[57] Unlike St Ninian's, the parish church, the chapel was situated in the town. It is likely to have been located on The Cross (**fig 29.7**), on the site where the Auld Kirk now stands; visual evidence suggests that the foundations of the Auld Kirk lie on earlier ones (*see* pp 20 and 59). The chaplain had a house and glebe in Kirkintilloch; this was probably the large house, called the 'Rood House', which stood opposite, at the top of Back Causeway (**fig 29.8**), a street which ran east off Cowgate. There were Latin inscriptions above the doorway and windows of the house, one of which read *Gloria Dei*.[58]

Kirkintilloch stood on a major route between Glasgow and Edinburgh. There was a ford over the Luggie at Oxgang, but, more importantly, there was a bridge over the Luggie Water beside the town (**fig 29.9**).[59] It is not known when the bridge was built, although by the close of the sixteenth century it was in a poor state of repair.[60] Often the burgh is encountered in documentary sources simply because of its situation on the highway. During their rebellion in 1489, the Earl of Lennox, his son Matthew Stewart and Lord Lyle held Dumbarton Castle. The accounts of the High Treasurer on 4 August record a payment to 'Barcar and ane odir gunnar', to pass from Linlithgow to Kirkintilloch to help bring home the guns.[61] James IV (1488–1513) visited and apparently drank in the burgh in 1501 and probably visited again when he stayed at Craigbarnet mansion house in the parish of Campsie in 1508 on his way to Glasgow.[62] Artillery is again recorded as passing through Kirkintilloch in October 1528, this time en route to Edinburgh.[63] French soldiers were quartered at Kirkintilloch in 1559 on their way to recovering the castle at Glasgow, returning to Kirkintilloch en route to Linlithgow and Edinburgh.[64]

At the close of the sixteenth century Kirkintilloch remained a small burgh, although very little can be said about the nature of the townscape at that period. The dwellings up Peel Brae towards the old castle are likely to have remained, but as the castle's importance diminished and the road presumably became more significant, the focus of the burgh shifted towards High Street, which extended at least as far as the Luggie. Southern development was limited and there were complaints that the parish church at the Old Aisle, which was south of the town, was too far removed and had no dwelling places near by.[65]

1600–1770

Urban setting

Considerably more information survives about Kirkintilloch from the seventeenth century, allowing a better picture of the burgh and its development to emerge. Earlier charters granted to the burgh were confirmed, although there were some disputes between the town and its feudal superiors, the Earls of Wigtown.[66] The structure of the burgh government can be determined: by the seventeenth century only proprietors of the lands known as the Newland Mailings could be burgesses. There were 33½ of these mailings, and ownership of half a mailing was qualification. The burgesses met annually to elect two bailies, one with jurisdiction for the east side of Luggie Water and the other for the west side. The bailies were empowered to hold courts, levy fines, imprison offenders or even banish them.[67] During the seventeenth century each bailie had the services of three or four burgesses for assistance, but from 1689 their status was improved in effect to that of town councillors.[68]

Documentary sources offer an insight into the town's layout by the seventeenth century. High Street extended down towards the Luggie Water and over it, and during the 1670s efforts were made to build a causeway with sand and stones on the east and west of the Luggie.[69] A sasine in 1660 records a house next to 'empty ground' on the east side of the Luggie,[70] but despite this, the east of the Luggie must have been important in the seventeenth century because separate bailies were elected for each side. In the Earl of Wigtown's 1670 charter eighteen individuals are listed as burgesses of the west side of the Water of Luggie and eighteen of the east side.[71] The development from High Street down Cowgate is also discernible. Properties are recorded on the east side of Churchgate, an earlier name for Cowgate, in 1664 and 1682.[72] Buildings at Townhead were also recorded, in a manner that suggests it was within the burgh but considered a separate area. In 1659 Elizabeth Henrie and her husband, William Henrie, inherited two tenements, with two barns and two barnyards and half an acre of arable land lying in Townhead, on the west side of the Luggie Water, within the burgh,[73] while in 1665 the marriage contract between John Guidding in Townhead, on the west side of Luggie Water, portioner of Kirkintilloch, and Euphemia Miller included houses, barns and a yard in Townhead.[74]

This township structure can be seen clearly in William Roy's map of 1747–55 (fig 4). Earlier maps, such as those by Blaeu, Moll and Gordon, do little more than record the burgh's existence.[75] Roy's map shows that the burgh was focused on High Street, the building activity and burgage plots stretching

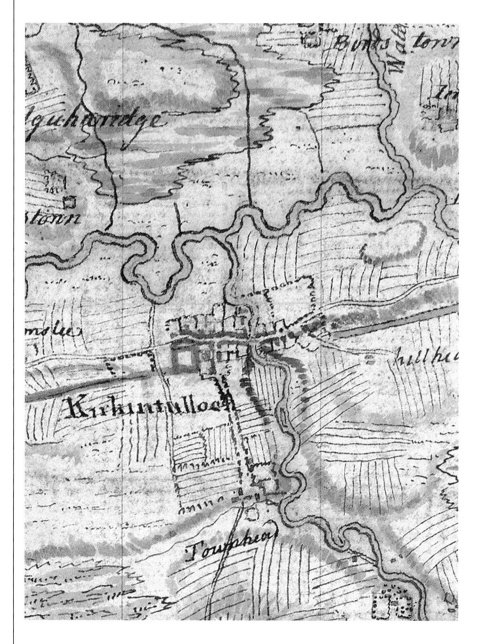

FIGURE 4:
Extract from William Roy's
Military Survey of Scotland,
1747–55 (By permission of
the British Library; Sheet X,
map C.9.b.5 3/2)

from the present-day West High Street eastwards along High Street over the
Luggie, into Eastside. The Peel apparently hindered development on the
south side of West High Street, but elsewhere building appears on both sides
of the road. The heaviest concentration was at the junction with Cowgate,
the area called The Cross. Houses were also scattered north of Cowgate and
further southwards at Townhead. The filling in of burgage plots seems to
have been minimal: there are frequent references to yards, waste land and
vacant pieces of land.[76] Regulations were repeatedly enacted to ensure the
'yaird dykes' were kept in good order, and to inhibit 'cloathes be layde on the

dykes'.[77] In one dispute James Frieland, tailor, and Alexander Stinson were fined and ordered to pay damages because their dyke was insufficient and had resulted in John Burnsyde, tailor, losing 20s worth of 'grein keall'.[78]

One of the few surviving buildings in the burgh which date from this period is St Mary's church, known as the Auld Kirk (NS 6521 7407; Category A-listed, **figs 5 & 29.3**). From the close of the sixteenth century there was a succession of complaints about the parish church at the Old Aisle (also known as Auld Aisle or Isle) (**fig 6**). In 1597 the bailies of Kirkintilloch complained to the Presbytery that the church was too far from the town and suggested that the chapel of St Mary in the town should be made into the parish church. Nothing came of this proposal, nor a similar one a decade later, despite its having the backing of the Earl of Wigtown and gaining the support of the Presbytery.[79] The church at the Old Aisle was also deemed unsatisfactory for those in the Cumbernauld district, who in 1621 petitioned parliament to have the barony of Lenzie made into two separate parishes.[80] The issue was only adequately addressed in 1642 when the Earl of Wigtown, his son and the bailies and burgesses of Kirkintilloch agreed that the parish church at the Old Aisle should be taken down and a new church built on the site of the chapel in the burgh. The church was to be paid for by the earl's tenants, and the bailies and burgesses of Kirkintilloch were to contribute 1000 merks.[81] This was accomplished without delay and a date stone on the south gable of the Auld Kirk gives the year of building as 1644. Since this new parish church was even further away for those in the eastern part of the parish, the Commissioners for the Plantation of Kirks decreed in 1649 that the parish of Lenzie should be divided into two new parishes, called Wester and Easter Lenzie, later renamed Cumbernauld and Kirkintilloch. Each was to have a separate parish church, Kirkintilloch utilising the one lately finished and Cumbernauld building a new one of its own.[82] The Auld Kirk at Kirkintilloch was built in the shape of a Greek cross, but had traditional Scottish crow-stepped gables and may have been built with stones from the ruins of the nearby castle.[83] By 1733 it was mentioned as having a slate roof.[84] In the 1830s, prior to major repairs, it held around 800 persons.[85] In the eighteenth century the kirk saw various secessions. In 1735 the Reverend William Fleming was appointed as minister for Kirkintilloch by the Earl of Wigtown, the patron, against the wishes of the parishioners, a number of whom attended the secession church of Ebenezer Erskine in Stirling. In 1765 they established the first secession congregation in Kirkintilloch, known as the Kirkintilloch Burgher Congregation, and a few years later built a church to the east of Cowgate adjacent to Back Causeway (**fig 29.10**). This building survived until the 1960s.[86]

The tolbooth of Kirkintilloch stood at The Cross (**fig 29.7**) until the early nineteenth century. It is not known when it was built, but references appear from the start of the burgh's first extant Court Book in 1659. The tolbooth was used for meetings of the burgh court and acted as a jail; in addition,

FIGURE 5:
Auld Kirk (By courtesy
of East Dunbartonshire
Information and Archives)

FIGURE 6:
Gateway to the 'Auld Isle',
2004 (Headland Archaeology)

important announcements were made at the tolbooth's door and the burgh's stocks stood outside it.[87] In the mid-eighteenth century the tolbooth was renovated to incorporate the parish school. Kirkintilloch had a parish school from an early date, standing, according to early nineteenth-century sources, on a piece of ground south of Kirkgate, but in 1748 the building was dilapidated. The land and materials were sold off to Andrew Graham and the money received was put towards the tolbooth's refurbishment, the school comprising the whole upper floor.[88] The tolbooth was demolished in 1813, to be replaced by the Town-house or 'Barony Chambers' (**fig 29.11**).[89]

In the seventeenth and eighteenth centuries, and probably long before, Kirkintilloch's market cross stood in front of the old tolbooth, and the locality is still known as 'The Cross' (**fig 29.7**). The burgh's markets and fairs were held at the market cross, and regulations were enacted to ensure fair trading there.[90] In addition, a regular lint market was held in Eastside from at least the eighteenth century.[91] In 1815 the cross was 'wantonly and maliciously' overturned by vandals. Presumably this was the same cross that had been standing for centuries; certainly contemporaries referred to it as the Old Cross Stone. The remnants of the cross were, 'for safety', placed in the bed of the Luggie, apparently near where the stream joins the Kelvin. No traces can now be found, but local reminiscences suggest the cross was 'an octangular pillar abundantly provided with steps and stones'.[92]

Only two domestic buildings from this period still stand in High Street, probably dating to the seventeenth or eighteenth centuries, although some have argued that they could date from the early nineteenth century. These are Westermains farm buildings on West High Street (listed Category B, **figs 7 & 29.12**) and the close at no. 18 West High Street (listed Categories B and 'C(S)', **fig 29.13**).[93] However, large numbers of buildings with typical seventeenth- and eighteenth-century architectural features – crow-stepped gables and steeply pitched roofs – were still evident in High Street, The Cross and Peel Brae in the late nineteenth century before they were demolished (**figs 3, 8 & 9**). These include the building at the corner of Cowgate and West High Street, identified as that referred to in a charter of 1670 as 'David Dalrumple's cors house' and the Black Bull Inn on High Street (**fig 29.14**), which held its licence from 1731.[94] There were fewer seventeenth- and eighteenth-century houses in Cowgate, although there were a number to the north of it, in particular the large three-storey building with small-paned windows, crow-stepped gables and a circular staircase usually referred to as the 'Old Post Office' (**figs 10, 11 & 29.15**), which was demolished in the early 1950s.[95] Townhead had few crow-stepped buildings, though old photographs feature two thatched ones with gables facing the street (**fig 12**).[96] The older buildings east of the Luggie are now gone, including little cottages with crow-stepped gables (**fig 13**) that were demolished in the nineteenth century, and a row of old cottages with crow-stepped gables that extended from the Luggie to Ledgate.[97]

FIGURE 7:
Westermains farm buildings
on West High Street, *c* 1975
(By courtesy of RCAHMS;
© Crown copyright
RCAHMS)

FIGURE 8:
Peel Brae, *c* 1880
(By courtesy of East
Dunbartonshire Information
and Archives)

FIGURE 9:
High Street, looking west,
1874 (By courtesy of East
Dunbartonshire Information
and Archives)

This townscape, limited in terms of extent and concentration, suggests Kirkintilloch was a small burgh, an impression supported by the low number of burgesses and bailies who served the town. The first clear evidence of the size of the population comes in the mid-eighteenth century. In 1755 Dr Webster estimated that there were 1696 residents in the entire parish.[98] The number in the town is harder to determine, but in 1751 the Reverend Doctor Erskine, then minister of Kirkintilloch, had calculated that there were 195 families in the town and 226 in the surrounding countryside. If a family is considered to contain four persons (an estimate used slightly later) then the population of the town was 780 and there were 904 in the countryside. This method suggests there were 1664 persons in the parish, which is sufficiently close to Dr Webster's estimates to give the calculation a degree of validity.[99]

FIGURE 10:
(above left) 'Old Post Office', Cowgate, c 1882, after installation of the Wallace Fountain in 1881 (By courtesy of East Dunbartonshire Information and Archives)

FIGURE 11:
(above right) The Old Post Office, photographed by I G Lindsay in 1937. The Fountain and a thatched house opposite have gone, and a phone box has arrived (By courtesy of RCAHMS; © Crown copyright RCAHMS)

FIGURE 12:
Townhead, looking north, c 1880. The thatched house belonged to the flax dresser Malcolm Fyfe (By courtesy of East Dunbartonshire Information and Archives)

Admittedly, these calculations do not include nonconformist religious groups such as Seceders and Quakers, but their numbers were few and do not alter the impression that the population of the burgh was very small.

Kirkintilloch as a routeway

Daniel Defoe, on his journeys in the early eighteenth century, did not mention Kirkintilloch, despite presumably passing through the burgh while travelling from Glasgow to Stirling, via Kilsyth.[100] The road upon which Kirkintilloch lies was described in 1790 as one of the great roads between Glasgow and Edinburgh.[101] From the close of the sixteenth century there were numerous efforts to maintain the route, especially the Kirkintilloch bridge over the Luggie. In 1598 the Convention of Royal Burghs gave a licence to the burgh of Glasgow to collect an impost at the bridge of Kirkintilloch for three years, the proceeds of which were to be used for its repair and upkeep. Each loaded horse was to pay 2d, each footman with a burden 1d, each horse, cow or ox 1d and every ten sheep 2d.[102] The following year the inhabitants of Kirkintilloch petitioned the privy council to do something about the bridge at Inchbelly (where the A803 now crosses the Kelvin) (**fig 1**) and the bridge of Kirkintilloch (**fig 29.9**) which was described as 'altogidder decayit and fallin doun'. The decayed condition of these bridges was seriously hindering movement to and from the western parts of the realm, and during bad weather was endangering life, livestock and merchandise, particularly herring and other goods from the west. So bad was the condition of these bridges and so crucial to travelling passage, that poor travellers and cadgers (packmen or itinerant hucksters) were willing to contribute towards the repair by paying duty for their usage. Consequently Johnne Stark, burgess of Edinburgh, was appointed to rebuild the Luggie (or Kirkintilloch) Bridge and repair Inchbelly Bridge. He was authorised to receive a toll of 2d at each bridge for every horse-load of goods over a three-year period, and these sums were to be applied for the building and repairs.[103]

In 1672, the bridge at Kirkintilloch was again described as 'decayit' As a result, the Earl of Wigtown built a bridge with three arches. In recompense the earl was allowed by Act of Parliament to exact 4d Scots from every ox, horse or cow; 4d for every ten sheep; and 8d for every loaded cart for the subsequent five years.[104] Shortly afterwards the bailies and burgesses of Kirkintilloch unanimously rejected an offer for the customs of Luggie Bridge, unless they had it upon easy terms and conditions.[105]

This bridge lasted barely 40 years, having collapsed by February 1713, following a great flood. The Earl of Wigtown, the justices of peace, heritors and freeholders in Dumbartonshire, and the magistrates of Glasgow, Stirling and others burghs adjacent to Kirkintilloch demanded a parliamentary bill for rebuilding, keeping and maintaining the bridge, and granted the Earl of Wigtown the duties and customs to that effect.[106] The only alternative trade route from Glasgow to Edinburgh or Bo'ness for carts and other merchandise during spates and bad weather was by the bridge of Calder, which was also dilapidated.[107] Presumably the bridge was rebuilt, but in October 1715 the Duke of Argyle, General and Commander in Chief of His Majesty's forces in North Britain, ordered the magistrates of Glasgow, Kirkintilloch and Kilsyth to make improvements to the bridge so as to allow cannons to cross. Between 18 October and 26 November 1715 Glasgow's council spent £404 0s 4d on timber, nails, carriage, and wages and provisions for masons, wrights, carters and others for Kirkintilloch bridge.[108] Glasgow's council certainly considered its own contribution significant, calling in May 1717 for its considerable investment to be protected by casting or paving the bridge and heightening the ledges, at its own expense.[109] In March 1720 there was a local bill for a toll for repairing the bridge of Inchbelle (Inchbelly) and the bridge and pavements of Kirkintilloch.[110] In January 1724 Glasgow's council was again concerned about the decaying state of the Kirkintilloch (Luggie) Bridge, which was likely to collapse, a situation it considered would be 'very prejudiciall' to the city. Meetings were to be arranged with trading merchants to consider what was to be done, and to confer with the Earl of Wigtown.[111] It is doubtful whether much action was taken, although a payment was made to John Craig, wright, for timber for Kirkintilloch Bridge.[112] In May 1727, when Glasgow's council made an agreement with Robert Henderson, mason in Stirling, to build Kirkintilloch Bridge, it was stipulated that it was to be 12 ft [3.7m] broad with ledges 3 ft [0.91m] high, with two arches. The mason was to pay for the stones, sand, lime and timber, although the timber and stone from the old bridge could be used. Each stone in the arch was to be at least 8 inches [0.2m] deep, and the bridge was to be finished by mid-September. In return Henderson was to be paid 1700 merks with an extra 100 merks if it was felt warranted.[113] Glasgow may well have resented its continued outlays on the bridge, for in 1734 the burgh successfully appealed to the Convention of Royal Burghs for power to compel Kirkintilloch to contribute to the upkeep of its bridge. The Convention gave Glasgow a licence to impose a toll for three years for its reparation and upkeep: 2d on each loaded horse, 1d per footman with a burden, 1d for each horse, cow or ox, 2d for every ten sheep.[114] Thereafter the bridge appears less frequently in the records. A picture of the bridge around 1880, before the late nineteenth-century alterations, may be deduced as showing the three arches it now has (**fig 13**), rather than the two stipulated in the 1727 plan.[115] This came about as the Luggie Bridge at Kirkintilloch was entirely renewed during the 1790s.[116]

In 1753 Glasgow was also complaining about the state of the principal roads to and from the burgh, including the 'high road leading from Inchbelly Bridge, through the town of Kirkintilloch … to the city of Glasgow'. It claimed the roads, of commercial and military significance, were in dire need of repair, impassable in winter for wheeled carriages and horses, and

FIGURE 13:
Eastside, looking west, including Luggie Bridge,
(a) *c* 1880 before its widening and (b) after widening in 1881 (By courtesy of East
Dunbartonshire Information and Archives)

that several bridges were precarious for travellers. Since for some reason the roads could not be repaired through the usual means appointed by laws and statutes, the city proposed erecting turnpikes and tollhouses in order to levy tolls to help pay for the roads' upkeep.[117]

As Glasgow's council emphasised, Kirkintilloch stood on a route of military importance. Indeed, in the seventeenth and early eighteenth centuries the burgh's involvement in national events was normally the result of this routeway. In 1653 Colonel Robert Lilburne wrote to Cromwell that Sir Arthur Forbes had gone to Kirkintilloch and plundered 'onely the poor congregated people and did noe more harme'.[118] The house of John Steven, merchant and indweller of Kirkintilloch, was burnt down by a sudden fire after a shot from an English soldier on 17 September 1660.[119] In 1678 the earls of Caithness, Strathmore and Airlie arrived in Kirkintilloch with Highland troops to suppress the Covenanters. The inhabitants of Kirkintilloch had to supply horses to transport the government's artillery, and the following year the town was quartering troops to fight Covenanters.[120] In 1689, 330 Danish troops were quartered in Kirkintilloch en route from Leith to Greenock for William, Prince of Orange's war in Ireland.[121] Again in 1690 troops were quartered and supplied at Kirkintilloch, because, the inhabitants claimed, their village lay on one of the greatest roads in the kingdom; this, they added, was a great burden on them.[122] It has already been noted that during the 1715 Jacobite rising the Duke of Argyle ordered that the bridge over the Luggie be improved so that cannons could cross it. The town was nearly burned down on 3 January 1746 by the Jacobite army, after a Kirkintilloch inhabitant shot one of the passing Highlanders. A threat to burn the town down was lifted only after a large fine was paid.[123]

Merchants and craftsmen

The road and bridge must have been important for commerce between Glasgow and the east coast, especially as Glasgow's trade expanded. It is not surprising that Glasgow was active in maintaining the road and bridge at Kirkintilloch. In the middle decades of the seventeenth century inhabitants from Glasgow, Edinburgh and Bo'ness had connections with Kirkintilloch. Inhabitants from these towns traded goods, owned property and had family ties in Kirkintilloch.[124] The overwhelming impression in the seventeenth century, however, is that the burgh's commerce was geared towards serving the local community. The main products sold in the market appear in a list of the small customs duties charged on goods coming to the town to be sold. In 1665 specific duties were levied on meal, cheese, salt, herring, hides, tallow, lead, yarn, lint, linen, coarse flax cloth and lintseed;[125] fairs may have attracted slightly more diverse commodities and consumers. There are indications that the market privileges were being abused. In 1648, Glasgow complained about the 'recent mercats of Kirkintilloch and the mercats of Kilsyth and Burnsyd', although the nature of the dispute is not given.[126] In 1669 Kirkintilloch paid 10d a year to the agent for the royal burghs to gain the right to trade outside the burgh.[127]

There are numerous references to the sale of lint and lintseed at Kirkintilloch in the seventeenth century[128] and from the eighteenth century, at least, regular lint markets were held at Eastside. This trade prospered in the eighteenth century as the Scottish linen industry expanded with the encouragement of the Board of Trustees for Fisheries and Manufacturers. Observers in the early nineteenth century remembered that 'lintseed Saturdays were formerly great marts for the sale of the commodity'.[129] The abnormal width of Eastside (**fig 13**) was apparently due to the market, 'the bailies taking care that sufficient width was left unbuilt upon for the purpose'.[130] Packhorses brought the lint to market and stood along the sides of Eastside and down Ledgate; the name 'Ledgate' is derived from the gangs of led horses coming regularly along it for the lint market. Lint was cultivated extensively across Scotland, and farmers brought it from Kilsyth, Fintry, Falkirk and the surrounding districts, although a large proportion of the lint seed sold in Kirkintilloch was imported from Holland and the Baltic. It was landed at Bo'ness and brought to Kirkintilloch by packhorse.[131]

Kirkintilloch merchants were active in the burgh's trade and seem to have been in a relatively privileged position. In 1680 all tradesmen who were not burgesses and freemen of Kirkintilloch were to pay an annual fee for the privilege of trading. Merchants were to pay 2 merks Scots, brewers 20s and the remainder 10s.[132] Seventeenth-century records show that weaving and textile production were important occupations in Kirkintilloch and the surrounding district. There were steeping ponds for flax on the higher reaches of the Luggie, and according to local tradition there were lint holes in the moss behind Waterside, where flax was steeped in stagnant water to loosen the fibres from the bark. The Burgh Court Book records a number of entries of flax steeping. In 1680 every man was to keep within his own 'mosse for watering of their lint' under a penalty of £5 and the loss of their lint.[133] In 1684 a complaint was made that the servant of John Burnsyde, Margaret Robertsoune, had left the lint of John Burnsyde in Patrick Gevan's 'peitt holl' against the acts of the court.[134] The Burgh Court Book documents various weavers and lesser numbers of walkers, listers (dyers), and tailors in Kirkintilloch, Townhead and the surrounding district.[135] A handful of testaments for weavers and tailors, or their spouses, survive from the middle decades of the seventeenth century.[136] Presumably, just as Kirkintilloch's lint market developed in the eighteenth century, the production of linen textiles in the district also expanded. By the middle of the seventeenth century, William Robertson, together with several Glasgow merchants, owned printfields in Woodside and Kirkintilloch. A great deal of the produce was sent to England.[137]

Apart from merchants and textile workers, the tradesmen listed in Kirkintilloch were brewers, cordiners, coopers, smiths, fleshers and wrights.

Other non-agrarian occupations include millers and butchers, as well as male and female servants.[138] Retailing of alcohol was also an important occupation: in 1756 thirteen persons were licensed to sell drink, including ten who were specifically listed as innkeepers.[139] All these were basic occupations to serve the town and its immediate hinterland.

The specialist traders and craft manufacturers in Kirkintilloch were probably also mainly concerned with servicing the local area. Agriculture was of fundamental importance to the burgh in the seventeenth and early eighteenth centuries, for this was a semi-agrarian burgh. It has been shown that only those with Newland Mailings, rather than those owning urban property, could become burgesses, and only burgesses could become bailies or serve on the town council. There are numerous references to barns and yards within the burgh,[140] and the burgh court spent a large proportion of time dealing with disputes over rural property and attempts to control livestock within the town.[141] In addition, there are references to coal extraction and significant peat cutting in the vicinity.[142]

Summary
In this period the documentary sources relating to Kirkintilloch become more numerous. Kirkintilloch was a small, semi-agrarian community whose commerce was geared towards the immediate hinterland. In the middle of the eighteenth century there were fewer than 800 inhabitants. The core of the burgh was focused on High Street, especially around The Cross. The burgh and its importance may have grown as Glasgow's commerce expanded, since it stood on an important east–west road, and, certainly in the eighteenth century, visitors from far afield attended the burgh's weekly lint market. New buildings were constructed, notably the Auld Kirk, and older ones were renovated, such as the tolbooth. The pace of change, however, was insignificant compared with what was to follow in the subsequent century.

1770–1900

Textile production at Kirkintilloch
The small, semi-agrarian community of Kirkintilloch changed dramatically from the end of the eighteenth century. The town's population burgeoned from around 800 in the 1750s, to 1531 in 1791, 4172 in 1828 and 8029 in 1881.[143] The physical appearance, economic base, transport infrastructure, town amenities and burgh government also underwent dramatic changes in a little over a hundred years. Observers were quick to write about the transformation of the town during their lifetimes. Two factors in particular had a profound and enduring impact on Kirkintilloch: the expansion of textile production and improvements in transport.

Kirkintilloch had a long tradition of textile production, and linen output may have increased in the late eighteenth century. In 1779 a lint mill was built at Waterside (**fig 1**) for 'scutching', to separate the fibre from the woody portion of the stalks of flax.[144] It was noted in the 1790s that considerable varieties and quantities of linen cloth were manufactured,[145] but linen became a less important component of the town's textile trade, and by the early nineteenth century Kirkintilloch's flax markets at Eastside were in decline. Contemporaries in the 1790s gave equal prominence to cotton production. This was a more recent development and would become the town's main industry in the middle of the nineteenth century.

In 1791 the Old Statistical Account recorded that a small cotton mill had recently been built near the confluence of the Luggie and Kelvin. This mill was owned by Sir John Stirling, whose two-storey house in Eastside still stands (**fig 29.16**).[146] The account also mentions that spinning was being done in the home, using newly introduced hand-machines. It went on to add that the industry was in a thriving condition and that the women in the parish were famous for their domestic spinning.[147] References to Kirkintilloch's spinning industry, however, are sparse, presumably partly because it was largely a female occupation. A 'ruin' indicated on the 1st and 2nd edition OS maps just north-west of the Glasgow Road bridge probably was the cotton mill. It would be interesting to know more about its importance in the burgh.

There can be little doubt that there was a rapid expansion in handloom weaving in Kirkintilloch at the same time as in other areas in lowland Scotland. Paisley entrepreneurs are credited with stimulating the employment of weavers in all towns and villages near Glasgow and Paisley.[148] Initially, silk gauze was manufactured in Kirkintilloch, but as its popularity diminished, lappets (muslins with raised floral decoration) became more favoured and developed into a local speciality. Lappets found a ready market in the East India trade; other varieties of cloth, such as purls (a gauze with lappeting on it) and victories (a sort of thin gauze web), were sent to South America.[149] Production was on a large scale: it was estimated that in 1791 there were 185 weavers in the town, although this probably only included the heads of households. This figure dwarfs the other listed occupations.[150] The growth in the number of weavers was impressive, the 1836 church commissioners' census recording 471 heads of families in the parish who were weavers.[151] The actual number of weavers, rather than simply the heads of household, was considerably higher. It was estimated that in 1835 there were 1600 weavers in Kirkintilloch, 2000 in 1839, the number peaking slightly later at 2400. In 1828 there were 1200 looms in the town and by 1838 there were 1955 plain and eight harness looms. Yet the number of handlooms across Scotland generally declined in this same period so Kirkintilloch was going against the trend and now had more handlooms than any other town in the west of Scotland except Glasgow or Paisley.[152] The weavers in Kirkintilloch mainly worked for

FIGURE 14:
Demolition of weaving
shops, Union Street, 1956
(By courtesy of East
Dunbartonshire Information
and Archives)

entrepreneurs or 'manufacturers' from Paisley or Glasgow, although by 1839 there were two large entrepreneurs in the district: Mr John Marshall and Mr Grey of Duntiblae each employed many hundreds of handloom operators. It was stated that during peak periods Mr John Marshall employed 1200–1400 weavers and even during depressions 500–800.[153]

As handloom weaving expanded, weaving shops were built. These weaving shops had dwelling houses adjoining or above them. Often the weaver owned the house and shop in which he lived and worked. Many parts of the town, notably Hillhead, Eastside, Freeland Place, streets off Cowgate (such as Union Street [**fig 14**], Victoria Street, Broadcroft and Kerr Street), and most of Townhead district were built for the weaving industry.[154]

Weaving was always susceptible to the vagaries of the trade cycle, but, more importantly, the powerloom was increasingly replacing handloom weaving across the country. Handlooms endured in Kirkintilloch for longer than in other communities (see **figs 31 & 32**), but eventually the competition took its toll.[155] By the 1870s it was reported that there was a great falling off in the handloom business, upon which the prosperity of the town had depended for many years.[156] There were only about thirty looms in Kirkintilloch by the

FIGURE 15:
Slimon's Mill: a north-lit weaving shed looking east–west, the natural light falling onto the
working areas of female powerloom weavers
(By courtesy of East Dunbartonshire Information and Archives)

FIGURE 16:
Slimon's mill looking down the pass from north to south, showing the preserve of the
male tenters who looked after the mechanical aspects of the looms (By courtesy of East
Dunbartonshire Information and Archives)

early twentieth century, and weaving shops were turned into dwelling houses instead.[157]

Powerlooms were introduced into Kirkintilloch at a relatively late date. The first was in Brodie's Mill which opened in the 1860s at Southbank Road, but it lasted only a few years before it burnt down. Another weaving mill, James Slimon & Co, was established at Kelvinside in 1867 (**figs 15 & 16**). Three years later it too burnt down, but it was rebuilt. By the early twentieth century the mill held 300 looms and over 200 girls were employed. It made shirting, skirting, zephyr and costume cloth, all predominantly for the American market.[158]

Transport developments

Kirkintilloch's location on a major road between Glasgow and the east coast has already been stressed. The route was improved when a bypass road was built north of High Street *c* 1805 (**fig 17**), as through traffic no longer had to strain to climb up to The Cross, which was especially important for horses. To help pay for the cost of the new road, a tollhouse was established in the acute angle between West High Street and Glasgow Road. The existing tollhouse at the foot of West High Street (Category B-listed, **figs 17 & 29.17**) was probably built in the middle of the nineteenth century, according to cartographic evidence.[159] Coal carts bound for Lennoxtown, however, apparently avoided the tollbar, by using a track beyond Westermains farm up West High Street called the old 'coal road'.[160] More improvements were made to the bridge over the Luggie (Category B-listed) when in 1881 it was significantly altered and widened.[161] A coach ran each day from Washington Inn (**figs 17 & 29.18**) in Glasgow Road, Kirkintilloch (Category C(S)-listed), to Glasgow, and there was also through passenger traffic between Glasgow and Edinburgh.[162] The coach service between Glasgow and Stirling, which went via Kirkintilloch and Kilsyth, was re-routed during an outbreak of cholera in Kirkintilloch in 1832.[163] Kirkintilloch was the first place in the west of Scotland to be hit by the outbreak and it killed 36 people in the burgh. It is likely to have come to Kirkintilloch via the Forth and Clyde Canal.[164]

The construction of the Forth and Clyde Canal (**fig 29.4**) had a major impact on Kirkintilloch. The canal was designed for small ocean-going vessels and stretched across the central belt of Scotland, considerably improving Kirkintilloch's accessibility. Work began at Grangemouth in 1768 and moved westwards. The first section, which extended as far as Kirkintilloch, was opened in 1773. It was considered to be near enough to Glasgow to make the carting of goods practicable.[165] Financial difficulties initially hindered expansion further to the west, but with financial assistance from the government, the canal eventually reached Bowling on the Clyde in 1790.[166]

The canal at Kirkintilloch was said to have cut through 'a green, undulating sward' of land.[167] A port was built at Hillhead (**fig 29.19**), east of Kirkintilloch

FIGURE 17:
Glasgow Road, c 1905,
looking east into West
High Street; on the right
is Washington Inn and
the old tollhouse is to the
left (By courtesy of East
Dunbartonshire Information
and Archives)

town centre, in 1773, because the aqueduct between there and the town was still incomplete. A temporary warehouse was erected in the 'cheapest manner' possible and the temporary nature of the port facilities at Kirkintilloch was stressed,[168] but the port endured. Until recently the sole remains, now also gone, were the red-brick houses which were formerly stables along the south bank of the wide part of the canal; horse-drawn vessels were the standard and only began to be replaced from the 1850s.[169] In 1774 an aqueduct (Category A-listed, **fig 29.5**) was built to carry the canal over the Luggie; later it would also carry the Campsie Branch railway (**fig 29**). It has been described as a handsome construction of solid masonry with wide arches spanning the river.[170] A bascule bridge was also constructed over the canal, connecting Townhead and Cowgate (**fig 29.21**). In 1778 Loch stated that Kirkintilloch was 'a small village on the side of the great canal. The town is increasing on this account'.[171] Indeed Charles Ross's map in 1777 (**fig 18**) shows that shortly after the canal opened at Kirkintilloch, buildings had already been erected on its banks to the south of Cowgate and the north of Townhead.

Kirkintilloch was a port of call for passenger boats. In the 1830s seven iron boats were used for passengers and 1932 paying passengers per month embarked at Townhead bridge in 1837.[172] Facilities for passengers were established beside Townhead Bridge in the 1840s, for example the Queen Hotel, more usually known as the Eagle Inn, which also had stables for the canal horses.[173] Passenger services declined heavily, however, after the Edinburgh and Glasgow Railway was opened in 1842.[174] Kirkintilloch also acted as a mid-way port catering for freight traffic through the canal. In the

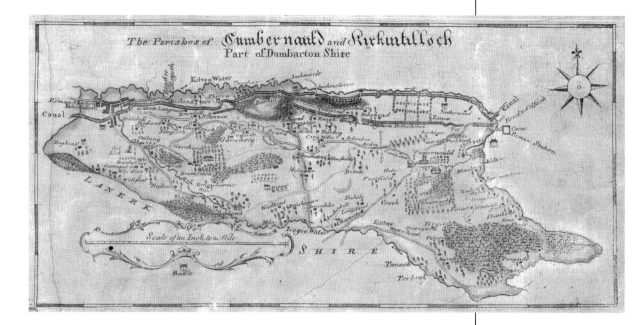

early nineteenth century the main commodities, in terms of revenue, were grain, sugar, coal, timber, pig iron, herring, coffee, cocoa and ironstone. In volumetric terms coal was the most significant, but it was a bulky, low-value commodity.[175] Following the construction of the Monkland and Kirkintilloch Railway (**fig 29.22**), which terminated at the canal in Kirkintilloch, the town also became important as a loading point, and this acted as a significant stimulus to manufacturing.[176]

The Monkland and Kirkintilloch Railway was opened to the public in October 1826, although part of it had been in use earlier. It ran to the Forth and Clyde Canal, terminating beside the canal in Southbank Road, where a station was built (**fig 29.22**). From an early date steam locomotives were used, rather than horses, and because of this it is sometimes regarded as the first proper railway in Scotland; the Dalkeith to Edinburgh Railway had opened few months earlier, but was not fully mechanised until 1845.[177] The main business of the Monkland and Kirkintilloch Railway was freight; passenger travel was of little significance and ceased entirely from the mid-nineteenth century. Coal was brought by rail from Monklands to the canal to be taken to Edinburgh and other east coast destinations. The distribution of pig iron from iron works in Monklands was also significant, although most was taken to Glasgow via the Monkland Canal. The railway and the canal were instrumental in tapping the valuable coal and iron mining districts of Lanarkshire, and both systems worked in tandem from an early date. In May 1826, before the railway was opened, the Forth and Clyde Canal committee decided to erect a temporary wharf beside the Kirkintilloch terminus.[178] Less than a decade later a canal basin (**fig 29.24**) was built at the expense of the Forth and Clyde Canal committee on ground belonging to the Monkland and

FIGURE 18:
A detail from Charles Ross's *Map of the shire of Dumbarton*, 1777 (Reproduced by permission of the Trustees of the National Library of Scotland)

Kirkintilloch Railway. Water was let in on 28 February 1835. This proved to be successful, for less than a year later it was reported that the greatest part of the articles carried along the railway were transferred at Kirkintilloch harbour into vessels navigating the Forth and Clyde Canal. The success was such that in 1841 the railway company contracted an extension of the canal basin.[179]

'New industries' at Kirkintilloch

The Forth and Clyde Canal and the Monkland and Kirkintilloch Railway were vital to Kirkintilloch's economy in the nineteenth century. Most of the industrial concerns established at the time were built on the banks of the canal to facilitate the movement of raw materials and finished products.

A small shipyard was set up by James Welsh; the precise date is not known but the first recorded ship was launched in 1782.[180] It would appear to have been a short-lived venture as buildings belonging to James Welsh cannot be traced beyond 1788. More importantly, a boat-building yard was established by Samuel Crawford on the south bank of the canal immediately to the west of Townhead Bridge in 1866 (**fig 29.4**). The following year, after only one ship had been launched, the yard passed to the brothers James and John Hay. The Hay brothers were already well established as shipping agents and traders on the canal: their father, William Hay, had a farm at Meiklehill, Hillhead, and ran a boat-owning business in the 1830s and 1840s. The yard was used mainly to maintain the firm's own large fleet, although repairs were also made to other firms' canal boats and occasionally, during lulls in maintenance and repairs, new vessels were built for the company. The yard expanded in the 1870s when its three sheds were replaced by a long shed containing workshops and plant, part of it two-storeyed, although a fire completely destroyed the shed and damaged the main building in 1903. A slip dock with sheds and wharfage was built on land east of the canal basin in the 1880s. By the early twentieth century the firm had 20–30 employees.

The canal and railway links were instrumental in stimulating an iron-founding industry in Kirkintilloch. From meagre origins the industry grew to significant proportions: only seven people were described as founders in the town in 1839, but by 1901 917 were engaged in the manufacture of metals, machines, implements and conveyances. The first iron foundry was the Kirkintilloch Foundry, more commonly known as the Old Foundry. This was established in the 1830s, just south of the canal aqueduct over the Luggie (**fig 29.25**). Initially it specialised in railway castings and later in heavy engineering castings. It continued until the end of the nineteenth century, when the buildings were taken over by F McNeill & Co for the manufacture of roof felting.[181] A second foundry was established in 1861. The Star Foundry, later officially renamed the South Bank Iron Works, was situated in Southbank Road close to the Monkland Railway (**fig 29.26**). It spread from its original 4.5 acres (1.8ha), to over 8 acres (3.25ha) at the start of the twentieth century.

The foundry was best known for drains, gutters, pipes, heating appliances and sanitary connections. Nearby in Southbank Road was the Basin Foundry (**fig 29.27**), established in 1872. Its main wares were kitchen ranges, grates and heating stoves, and by the start of the twentieth century it employed 80–90 men. The best known foundry in Kirkintilloch was the Lion Foundry (**fig 29.28**), on the north side of the canal across from the Old Foundry, which opened in 1880 and soon gained a good reputation for making ornamental castings, gates, railings, fountains, shelters and bandstands. The Perry Bandstand (**fig 29.29**) and the Hudson Fountain (**fig 19**) (both listed Category C(S)) in Peel Park, gifted to the town at the start of the twentieth century, were manufactured by the Lion Foundry. By the early twentieth century the foundry covered 5 acres (2ha) and employed around 500 men and boys.[182]

Other industries in Kirkintilloch were stimulated by, and situated near, the main transport facilities, including various timber firms and mills on the bank of the canal.[183] In 1839 120 printers, mechanics and labourers were employed at the Bellfield Print Works, on the north bank of the canal.[184] In the second half of the century the site was used for the manufacture of fertilisers and chemical products, while across the canal in Southbank Road stood the Forth and Clyde Chemical Company.[185] In 1882 the Nickel Works were started by the New Caledonia Mines Company (**fig 29.30**) on the south bank of the canal, just beyond the burgh boundary. Ore was partially refined at Kirkintilloch and then sent to refineries in England, France and Germany.[186] The improved transport facilities and demand from local industry also stimulated coal-mining. Most coal-mining was to the east of the town. Small pits were sunk at Saddler's Brae, Langmuir, Braes-o'-Yetts and Solsgirth during the mid-nineteenth century, with the largest collieries at Meiklehill and Woodilee.[187] In addition, stone, gravel and sand were quarried in the locality.[188]

In 1848 a further railway came to Kirkintilloch, with the completion of the Campsie branch of the Edinburgh and Glasgow Railway (**fig 29.20**),[189] which had a station at Eastside and a bridge over that road to the west of Ledgate.[190] This was a more passenger-orientated line than the Monkland and Kirkintilloch Railway. There was a rash of suburban railway schemes in the 1880s, with Kirkintilloch no exception. Numerous stone-built villas (**fig 20**) were constructed for middle-class residents, especially in the Westermains and Bellfield areas of the town.[191]

The services in the town changed as the population rose, transport improved, new industries developed and wealth increased. Some trades and industries diminished, however, during the nineteenth century. A decline in the number of stocking makers, saddlers and coopers in the first half of the century was probably due to better supplies coming from Glasgow.[192] In the second half of the century, likewise, distilling and silk hat-making disappeared from the burgh. The glory days of the Eastside lint market were considered

The Hudson Fountain in Peel Park was made in Kirkintilloch by the Lion Foundry. Robert Hudson was a founder of Lion Foundry and this fountain toured trade fairs and exhibitions before installation here. There are others of the type in Kilsyth and Tomintoul (By courtesy of East Dunbartonshire Information and Archives)

a thing of the past by the 1830s.[193] At the start of the twentieth century it was noted that the main attractions at the fairs were side-shows and merry-go-rounds; no one thought of going to fairs to buy merchandise, or to take cattle or produce for sale.[194] Instead, there were more permanent shops: in the 1830s these included large numbers of merchants, grocers, bakers and butchers.[195] The burgh was well served with inns and alehouses, with about 40 in the parish in the 1830s.[196] Banks began to be established in the nineteenth century, and a significant number were operating in the second half of that century.[197]

The poor were not numerous in the parish in the late eighteenth century.[198] In the 1830s it was also noted that despite the rapidly increasing population, the rise in trade and manufacturing ensured that no poor rate had been imposed by law until a few years previously.[199] During cyclical downturns in trade poverty was more prevalent,[200] but generally it was not a major problem in the town. There was a poorhouse in Southbank Road, which in the 1880s had only two regular inmates (the two-storey building still exists; **fig 24, inset 2, & fig 29.47**).[201] The town's buildings and amenities were, however, struggling to cope with the rising population.

Urban growth and change
The expansion of the town's population and wealth is reflected in the construction and major repair of public buildings in the nineteenth

FIGURE 20: Alexandra Street, looking east to the predecessor to St David's Memorial Park Church, 1904 (By courtesy of East Dunbartonshire Information and Archives)

century. The Barony Chambers, also known as the Town-house and the Steeple (NS 6528 7399, Category B-listed, **figs 21 & 29.11**), were opened in 1815. Built on the site of the old tolbooth, at the junction of High Street and Cowgate, it had three separate apartments: the ground floor had a court hall and two small prison cells, the first floor contained a council room, and the upper floor a school, known as the 'steeple school'. From an early date the steeple housed a bell and a clock, which have been repaired and replaced on a number of occasions. The steeple bell is now in the Auld Kirk Museum. By 1860 the whole building was in need of extensive repairs. The Barony Chambers were replaced by the opening of the Town Hall (Category B-listed) on Union Street (**fig 29.31**) in September 1906.[202] There had been no real Town Hall in the nineteenth century. The Black Bull Inn (**fig 29.14**), on High Street, had been the principal hall in the town, a mantle which was transferred to the Temperance Hall in Alexandra Street (**fig 29.32**), built in 1872, although it was also inadequate.[203]

By the nineteenth century St Mary's church, or the Auld Kirk, was showing its age. In the 1830s the Reverend Adam Forman[204] wrote that the parish church was in a dilapidated state:

> the walls were time-worn and ungainly; the timbers in general fragile and insufficient; the galleries inconvenient and crazy, one of them having been lately taken out in case of the danger of it coming down at an inconvenient season; the seating was fast crumbling into ruins; the walls outside were filled up with dust ... the walls and flooring, of course, intolerably damp.[205]

Attempts to have a new church built were rejected on the grounds of cost. At the Court of Session it was shown that a new church would cost £1280, whereas repairs to make the church serviceable for 25–35 years would cost £660. Consequently the church underwent major repairs and subsequent renovation in 1890 extended its existence further.[206] Despite the alterations, however, the church was still too small and it finally ceased being the parish church in 1914, when the new St Mary's church (listed Category B, **fig 29.33**) was opened at the south of Cowgate, to take its place.[207] The Auld Kirk was thereafter used as a Sunday School and has been the town museum since 1961.

The late eighteenth and nineteenth centuries saw a variety of other churches built in Kirkintilloch. The Kirkintilloch Burgher Congregation, later known as the 'Marshall Church' (**fig 29.10**) after their minister, the Reverend Andrew Marshall (1802–54), moved in 1873 to a new church: St Andrew's Free Church. Situated in Townhead, the church was built in Gothic style with a tall spire. Various amalgamations eventually resulted in a union with St David's in Ledgate (originally built in 1837 as an extension of the Church of Scotland,

to help relieve overcrowding) and the decision to build a new church, later St Columba's. St Andrew's Church became the Volunteer Drill Hall, before being demolished in 1967; St David's is still standing. Other churches built in the nineteenth century include: St David's Free Church in Alexandra Street, 1845; Park Church in Kerr Street, 1855; and the Baptist Hall at the top of Regent Street, 1888. During the nineteenth century Irish Catholic labourers and their families settled in Kirkintilloch in increasing numbers. Initially they had to walk to Lennoxtown to celebrate Mass, but from 1875 services were conducted in a small hall built in Union Street. In 1893 the Holy Family and St Ninian's Roman Catholic Church (Category B-listed) was built in Union Street (**fig 29.34**). Built of Dumfries red sandstone, it was designed by the famous London firm of Pugin and Pugin.[208]

It has already been mentioned that the Barony Chambers contained the parish school, also known as the Steeple School. A house for the schoolmaster was built adjacent to it on the West High Street frontage (which in later years served as the Salvation Army Hall). There were various fee-paying schools in the town; these included Sergeant Begbie's school in Townhead, Cowgate Subscription School, John Street School in Hillhead, Kerr Street School, Freeland Place School, Montgomery's School in Beehive Close, Townhead, the Subscription School in Waterside that bears a plaque recording its erection in 1839, and a seminary for young ladies in Eastside. In the middle of the nineteenth century low-fee schools began to be established, such as a local Industrial Society School in 1853, an Industrial School off Union Street which was later moved to the Cowgate/Broadcroft corner, and in 1854 Oswald School on the corner of Glasgow Road and Campsie Road. The 1872 Education Act required school boards to take over the running of parish schools. New schools were opened at Lairdsland in 1875 and Townhead in 1890 which received pupils from Steeple School, Cowgate Industrial School and Oswald School. In 1874 the first Roman Catholic school was opened in Kirkintilloch in Union Street; another replaced it on the same street in 1895.[209]

From the late eighteenth century Kirkintilloch's economic base, transport infrastructure, and townscape changed dramatically. The burgh's population rose five-fold between 1791 and 1881. Such rapid growth in a short time inevitably led to serious problems with drainage, sanitation, water supply, housing conditions and streets within the town. Simply adding more houses left the town with unpaved and unlit streets, no system of drainage and without sanitary supervision.[210] Kirkintilloch's old town council, elected by the proprietors of Newland Mailings, became increasingly irrelevant and, because their revenue was restricted to small amounts from casualties, the council was financially powerless.[211] From the 1830s a second council, the Commissioners of Police, began to operate in the town alongside the old town council. A fifth of the Commissioners of Police were appointed by the old town council and the remainder were elected by those occupying premises with a yearly value of £10 and above. Their activities were financed by an assessment on property owners and tenants in the burgh. Despite having wide potential powers, their initial activities were confined mainly to providing security and lighting.[212] In 1871, however, the provisions of the 1862 General Police and Improvement Act were adopted. The old town council no longer had any involvement in appointing Commissioners, and the Commissioners of Police became more active and took on much wider responsibilities and greater power. In 1901 they officially redesignated themselves 'Kirkintilloch Town Council'. The old, and by then hopelessly obsolete, town council, elected by the proprietors of Newland Mailings, ceased to exist after 1908.[213]

In the 1830s the Commissioners of Police were looking for suitable sites on which to build a municipal gasworks, but in fact in 1838 a private company, the Kirkintilloch Gas Light Company, established a gasworks in Canal Street (**fig 29.35**).[214] At the same time street lamps were introduced.[215] The Commissioners purchased the Company in 1878 for £14,000. Attempts were made to improve the site, but there was no room for expansion so a new site at Back o' Loch (**fig 1**) was purchased and new gasworks were opened in 1908.[216]

A pressing concern in the town was the provision of running water. Previously wells fed by underground springs were used, but they were completely inadequate for the needs of the growing population and were often situated close to open sewers. There were only two public wells, one at Townhead and the other in Cowgate, with the pump lever for the Townhead well removed and made available only at certain times of the day.[217] There were also several private and semi-private wells, two near the Luggie Bridge, one at Braehead and another in Peel Park, which was described in 1856 as 'a well faced with stone', with a private spring on the site.[218] Another private spring called the 'The Spout' was on the site of the old gasworks.[219] In droughts, water from the River Luggie was utilised.[220] To improve the supply of water a waterworks was opened in 1874, water from the Corrie Burn in the Kilsyth Hills flowing into a 180,000-gallon storage tank from whence it was piped to the town. There were further improvements in 1881–85 when the Woodburn Reservoir was constructed, and in 1905 when the Corrie Reservoir was completed.[221]

Sanitation in the town was also a cause for considerable concern. A report on 14 March 1872 to the Board of Supervision noted the deplorable conditions. Inspections in Townhead, Blackhall, Hillhead, Eastside, Ledgate and West High Street showed deficiencies everywhere: 'ashpits and accumulations of manure abounded in all directions, open drains (carrying raw sewage in some instances) were led directly into the neighbourhood of wells supplying a considerable population'.[222] In 1875 it was resolved that the local authority should intervene to take care of the dungheaps and middens all over the town.

Between 1875 and 1914, moreover, there was considerable construction of drains and sewers throughout the town. On 20 December 1888 a purification plant was opened at Dryfield on the Kelvin.[223]

At the start of the nineteenth century a writer stated that 'the houses were constructed, in most cases, of rough stone, lime and with thatched roofs'.[224] Many dwellings in Kirkintilloch, especially the older ones, were in an appalling state. There was congestion, such as at Back Causeway,[225] disrepair of houses, poor internal conditions and many dwellings which were badly drained and prone to flooding.[226] From the late nineteenth century the civic authorities intervened: in 1885 the burgh surveyor was instructed to see that all thatched roofs due for repair were reroofed in slate,[227] and, more importantly, older properties were demolished. In 1904, the row of old houses on the south side of High Street was to be removed, and the *Kirkintilloch Herald* reported that 'another eyesore will be removed from that quarter of the town'.[228] It has already been noted that numerous seventeenth- and eighteenth-century buildings in West High Street, High Street, Eastside, Cowgate, and Townhead – the older areas of the town – were demolished in the late nineteenth and early twentieth centuries.

The roads in Kirkintilloch were in a lamentable condition, despite eight tollbars in and around the town in the 1850s.[229] From the 1880s the town council took over responsibility for the making, repairing and control of roads.[230] This led to the disappearance of tollbars in the town and an improvement in the roads. Roads were widened at The Cross and Townhead in March 1883,[231] while an observer in the late nineteenth century marvelled that pavements were now universal and had well-made kerbs.[232]

To commemorate Queen Victoria's Diamond Jubilee in 1897, the Commissioners of Police purchased the 'unfeued lands of Peel', which were then a dairy farm, and converted them into a public park. As space was limited it was left as an open space for the enjoyment of the public, rather than having extensive walkways and flowerbeds, although a bandstand and drinking fountain (**fig 19**) were gifted and erected in the park shortly after it opened.[233]

Summary

Kirkintilloch witnessed great changes in the period after 1770, as the population rose and transport, trade and industry developed. The townscape altered dramatically as a result. In particular, weaving shops were built in many new locations in the early part of the nineteenth century; the canal was the focus for a number of industrial concerns, especially after the Monkland and Kirkintilloch Railway was built; large suburban houses were built in the late nineteenth century; various public amenities were started; and older parts of the housing stock were destroyed. Little wonder writers at the time frequently wrote about the changes experienced in their lifetime, and how the town was now scarcely recognisable.[234] Visitors, however, were very disparaging about its appearance. One wrote in 1842 that 'it is an irregularly built, strangely arranged, confused looking little town, conveying by its aspect the idea of such entire devotement to trade and manufacture as precludes nearly all attention to the graces of exterior appearance'.[235] This refrain was echoed throughout the century.[236]

The twentieth century

The population of Kirkintilloch continued to grow rapidly in the twentieth century, reaching 14,826 in 1951 and 24,601 in 1969,[237] but the trades and industries upon which it had prospered in the previous century decayed and disappeared.

The amount of freight carried on the Forth and Clyde Canal fell heavily from the late nineteenth century as coasting vessels grew too big to use the canal, and industrial concerns next to the canal closed. Especially significant was the increased competition from railways and, later, road transport. The canal was finally closed on 1 January 1963, after freight declined dramatically following the Second World War, and the canal basin was filled in.[238] Three years later both of Kirkintilloch's railway lines were closed.[239] The Forth and Clyde Canal, however, has recently reopened as a leisure facility and a new bridge was opened at Kirkintilloch in May 2000.

The weaving mill of James Slimon & Co closed in 1930. The buildings were taken over and adapted by M & C Switchgear, manufacturers of electrical switch and control gear for mines.[240] Boat-building flourished in the first two decades of the century before collapsing. In 1902 a new boat-building firm, Peter McGregor and Sons, opened in the canal basin (**fig 29.24**). There was plenty of room at the site for berths for launching and fitting out, and five building berths were available.[241] An estimated 118 puffers, tugs and barges were built at the yard before difficulties led to its closure in 1921.[242] The Hay Brothers' yard (**fig 29.23**) also experienced difficult times from the 1920s, but it struggled on until just after the closure of the Forth and Clyde Canal in 1963. Today little remains of the yard.[243] The Star and Lion iron foundries remained operational for most of the century, the latter making the famous red telephone kiosks, before both closed in the early 1980s.

The 1960s saw industrial development away from the canal basin. As part of the Glasgow overspill project, Glasgow firms were encouraged to erect factories in Kirkintilloch, while Kirkintilloch town council agreed to build houses for families on the Glasgow Corporation waiting list. Industrial estates were laid out at Woodilee, Old Mill Park and Broomhill. New firms certainly were established, but few were as extensive as had been hoped.[244] The overspill project did, however, result in the construction of many homes in the town, in both the rented and private sectors. This was in addition to an extensive programme of council house construction dating back to the Back o' Loch scheme in the 1920s. Prior to the Second World War 1251 council houses were erected and this number increased to 2213 between 1946 and 1955.[245]

The construction of new houses, buildings and roads throughout the twentieth century culminated in the removal of many of the few surviving structures of antiquity. For instance, the last thatched property in the burgh, nos 69–71 Hillhead Road, which dated from 1793, was removed in 1947,[246] while the road widening at The Cross in 1952 led to the old post office being demolished. In more recent times, tenements at The Cross have been replaced by the new William Patrick Library, which opened in 1994 (**fig 29.2**).[247] Townhead is said to have been largely rebuilt since 1900,[248] and the bridge at Townhead was replaced twice during the twentieth century. The building of a relief road in the 1980s, New Lairdsland Road, running parallel to Cowgate, had a major impact on the townscape, including alterations to access roads such as Catherine Street. So extensive were the changes that it has been said that the face of Kirkintilloch underwent a total metamorphosis in the twentieth century. By the middle of the century even the burgh's guidebook noted a 'dearth of historic buildings'.[249] Today, the biggest group of dwelling houses over a century old comprises some villas in the Westermains and Bellfield area.[250] With just a little of antiquity remaining, it is perhaps fitting that this burgh, which has changed and adapted so often during its history, should be continuing to do so.

Notes

1   J Horne, 'General expansion', in Horne, *Kirkintilloch*, 5; J Fletcher, 'The burgh and parish of Kirkintilloch', in M S Dilke and A A Templeton (eds), *The Third Statistical Account. Vol vi, The County of Dunbarton* (Glasgow, 1959), 284

2   D J Breeze, *The Northern Frontier of Roman Britain* (London, 1982), 46

3   A S Robertson (revised by L Keppie), *The Antonine Wall: A Handbook to the Surviving Remains* (Glasgow, 2001), 96

4   A S Robertson, 'Miscellanea Roman-Caledonica', *Proc Soc Antiq Scot*, xcvii (1963–64), 180–2

5   For extensive discussions see G MacDonald, *The Roman Wall in Scotland* (Oxford, 1934), 289–96; T Dalrymple Duncan, 'Antiquities', in Horne, *Kirkintilloch*, 26–32

6   MacDonald, *Roman Wall*, 292; Robertson and Keppie, *Antonine Wall*, 97–8

7   MacDonald, *Roman Wall*, 292; Robertson, 'Miscellanea Roman-Caledonica', 184–5; D Martin, *The Story of Kirkintilloch* (SDLM, 1987), 4–6; Robertson and Keppie, *Antonine Wall*, 96

8   Breeze, *Northern Frontier*, 123–4

9   Horne, 'General expansion', 6–7

10   T Johnston, *Old Kirkintilloch* (Kirkintilloch, 1937), 2; A O Anderson (ed), *Early Sources of Scottish History, 500–1286* (Edinburgh, 1922), i, 97, 118–19

11   W J Watson, *History of the Celtic Place-names of Scotland* (Edinburgh, 1926), 348; MacDonald, *Roman Wall*, 290

12   *RRS*, ii, no. 501; G S Pryde, 'Two Burgh Charters, Kirkintilloch, 1211–1214, and Rothesay 1401', *Scottish Historical Review*, xxix (1950), 64–8

13   MacDonald, *Roman Wall*, 291

14   Martin, *Story of Kirkintilloch*, 10

15   Horsley, J, *Britannia Romana of the Roman Antiquities of Britain* (London, 1732)

16   T Johnston, *Old Kirkintilloch* (Kirkintilloch, 1937), 7

17   Fletcher, 'Burgh and parish', 285

18   Dalrymple Duncan, 'Antiquities', 37–8; Martin, *Story of Kirkintilloch*, 57; D Martin, *Kirkintilloch in Old Picture Postcards* (Zaltbommel, 1985), no. 12

19   MacDonald, *Roman Wall*, 292

20   MacDonald, *Roman Wall*, 293

21   Horne, 'General expansion', 18

22   Dalrymple Duncan, 'Antiquities', 38

23   Johnston, *Old Kirkintilloch*, 4; D Martin, *The Comyns at Kirkintilloch* (East Dunbartonshire Council, 2003), 1

24   I B Cowan (ed), *Parishes of Medieval Scotland* (SRS, 1967), 121; *RRS*, ii, no. 528; Dalrymple Duncan, 'Antiquities', 38–9; Martin, *Story of Kirkintilloch*, 7–8

25   Cowan, *Parishes*, 121; Martin, *Story of Kirkintilloch*, 12–13

26   Martin, *Story of Kirkintilloch*, 12–13; W Sunter, 'Ecclesiastical history', in Horne, *Kirkintilloch*, 84–5

27   Sunter, 'Ecclesiastical history', 85

28   C Innes, *Origines Parochiales*, 2 vols (Edinburgh, 1851–54), i, 49; Sunter, 'Ecclesiastical history', 85; Dalrymple Duncan, 'The House of Fleming', Horne (ed), *Kirkintilloch*, 231

29   Sunter, 'Ecclesiastical history', 89

30   J Irvine, *The Book of Dumbartonshire. Vol II, Parishes* (Edinburgh, 1879), 391

31   Dalrymple Duncan, 'Antiquities', 39

32   *ibid*, 40

33   J Gifford and F A Walker, *The Buildings of Scotland: Stirling and Central Scotland* (London, 2002), 571; Martin, *Old Picture Postcards*, no. 47

34   *Rotuli Scotiae in Turri Londinensi et in Domo Capitulari Westmonasteriensi Asservati*, 2 vols, ed D Macpherson *et al* (1814–19), i, 35

35   F J Watson, *Under the Hammer: Edward I and Scotland, 1286–1306* (East Linton, 1998), 140–1

36   Johnston, *Old Kirkintilloch*, 7. In September Sir William le Frauncey's forces in the castle amounted to 27 men at arms and 60 foot, including 20 crossbowmen. Between November and December the garrison contained 27 knights and men at arms, 2 smiths, 1 watchman, an *attillator*, 19 *balistens* and 19 archers (*CDS*, ii, 340; v, 175)

37   J Stevenson (ed), *Documents Illustrative of the History of Scotland 1286–1306* (Edinburgh, 1870), ii, 448; *CDS*, ii, 341

38 Horne, 'General expansion', 8

39 *CDS*, v, 185

40 *Scots Peerage*, ii, 257

41 *CDS*, v, 183–4

42 R Nicholson, *Scotland: the Later Middle Ages* (Edinburgh, 1989), 72

43 Dalrymple Duncan, 'Antiquities', 34

44 *CDS*, iii, 23

45 *CDS*, iii, 32

46 *CDS*, iii, 46

47 Dalrymple Duncan, 'Antiquities', 34

48 *ibid*, 39; *RMS*, i, no. 80

49 Martin, *Story of Kirkintilloch*, 14; T. Watson, *Kirkintilloch, Town and Parish* (Glasgow, 1894), 15

50 T Dalrymple Duncan, 'The house of Comyn', in Horne, *Kirkintilloch*, 227

51 G S Pryde (ed), *The Burghs of Scotland: A Critical List* (Oxford, 1965), no. 97; *RMS*, i, no. 466; the date is given as 13 May 1375 in *Scots Peerage*, viii, 534

52 Johnston, followed by Martin, refers to two bailies of Kirkintilloch being listed in 1363 – Johnne Miller and Johnne Cunninbrae – but elsewhere the date is given as 8 February 1563–64. Johnston, *Old Kirkintilloch*, 13; Martin, *Story of Kirkintilloch*, 14; Innes (ed), *Origines Parochiales*, i, 504

53 Watson, *Kirkintilloch*,15; Innes (ed), *Origines Parochiales*, i, 49

54 Watson, *Kirkintilloch*, 148. For the king's confirmation see *APS*, ii, 317

55 *Kirk Ct Bk*, pp li–lii and note on p xliv; Pryde, *Burghs*, no. 207

56 *RMS*, i, 643; Martin, *Story of Kirkintilloch*, 13; Innes (ed.), *Origines Parochiales*, i, 49; Sunter, 'Ecclesiastical history', 85

57 Martin, *Story of Kirkintilloch*, 13

58 Watson, *Kirkintilloch*, 49, 175

59 Horne, 'General expansion', 18

60 *RPC*, 1st ser, vi, 24

61 *TA*, i, 117

62 *TA*, ii, 113; Horne, 'General expansion', 10

63 *TA*, iv, 228

64 *The Historie of Scotland wrytten in Latin by Jhone Leslie and translated by James Dalrymple*, 3 vols, ed E G Cody (Scottish Text Society, 1885–90), ii, 428; Horne, 'General expansion', 9; *TA*, xi, 18. This last reference gives the date for provisioning the French army as March 1559/60

65 Martin, *Story of Kirkintilloch*, 14, 20

66 D Murray, *Early Burgh Organisation in Scotland. Vol II, Rutherglen, Lanark, Prestwick, Newton-upon-Ayr, Ayr* (Glasgow, 1932), note 1 on p 208

67 *OSA*, ix, 77

68 Martin, *Story of Kirkintilloch*, 19

69 *Kirk Ct Bk*, 36–7, 39, 44, 83

70 *ibid*, 146

71 Watson, *Kirkintilloch*, 149–50

72 *Kirk Ct Bk*, 7, 121

73   *ibid*, 3–4

74   EDA, GD85/1/13, Papers found in Westermains, Kirkintilloch

75   NLS, WD3B/28, J Bleau, 'The Province of Lennox' (1654); NLS, EMS. b.2.1(18), H Moll, 'Shire of Lenox [ie Lennox] or Dunbarton' (1745); NLS, Adv. MS.70.2.10 (Gordon 50), R & J Gordon 'Sterlinshyr and Lennox' (*c* 1636–52)

76   For example, *Kirk Ct Bk*, 3–4, 6–7, 121, 146; EDA, GD85/1/11, 13, 20; Watson, *Kirkintilloch*, 151; D Patrick, 'Burghal development', in Horne, *Kirkintilloch*, 45

77   *Kirk Ct Bk*, 30, 63, 94

78   *ibid*, 133

79   Sunter, 'Ecclesiastical history', 96–7; Martin, *Story of Kirkintilloch*, 20

80   Dalrymple Duncan, 'Antiquities', 39

81   Martin, *Story of Kirkintilloch*, 20–1

82   *ibid*, 21

83   Dalrymple Duncan, 'Antiquities', 35

84   Horne, 'General expansion', 19

85   *NSA*, viii, 205

86   Martin, *Story of Kirkintilloch*, 39; Sunter, 'Ecclesiastical history', 108

87   *Kirk Ct Bk*, 4, 6, 10, 57, 59, 76, 88

88   RCAHMS, *Tolbooths and Town-houses: Civic Architecture in Scotland to 1833* (Edinburgh, 1996), 127; Patrick, 'Burghal development', 45–8; Horne, 'General expansion', 23

89   A Stewart, 'Schools and schoolmasters', in Horne, *Kirkintilloch*, 139; Martin, *Story of Kirkintilloch*, 36; RCAHMS, *Tolbooths*, 127

90   *Kirk Ct Bk*, 8

91   *NSA*, viii, 210

92   Dalrymple Duncan, 'Antiquities', 37, note on p 272; Martin, *Story of Kirkintilloch*, 25–6

93   These buildings are considered to date from the seventeenth and eighteenth centuries in Martin, *Story of Kirkintilloch*, 56, but they are given as being from the early nineteenth century in Gifford and Walker, *The Buildings of Scotland*, 574

94   Martin, *Story of Kirkintilloch*, 56–7; Martin, *Old Picture Postcards*, no. 4

95   Martin, *Old Picture Postcards*, no. 16; Fletcher, 'Burgh and parish', 292

96   Martin, *Story of Kirkintilloch*, 58

97   J Hillis, *Life in a Scottish Country Town in the Victorian era. Personal Reminiscences: Kirkintilloch, Lenzie, Auchinloch* (Kirkintilloch, 1940)

98   *OSA*, ii, 281

99   *NSA*, viii, 189; *Scottish Population Statistics, including Webster's Analysis of Population, 1755*, ed J G Kyd (SHS, 1952), 35

100   D Defoe, *A Tour Through the Whole Island of Great Britain*, eds P N Furbank and W R Owens (New Haven, 1991), 332

101   *OSA*, ix, 77

102   *RCRB*, ii, 36–7

103   *RPC*, 1st ser, vi, 24, 619

104   *APS*, viii, 97
105   *Kirk Ct Bk*, 46–7
106   *Glas Recs*, iv, 495
107   *ibid*, 515–16
108   *ibid*, 566, 584, 593, 631. NAS, E640/25/35, Forfeited Estates Papers 1715, Kilsyth
109   *Glas Recs*, iv, 612
110   NAS, GD45/1/215, Dalhousie Muniments, 3 March, 1720
111   *Glas Recs*, v, 182
112   *ibid*, 185–6
113   *ibid*, 278–9
114   Horne, 'General expansion', 12–13
115   Strathkelvin District Libraries, *A Walk Through Kirkintilloch's Past* (SDLM, 1982), 7–8
116   D Martin, pers comm
117   *Glas Recs*, vi, 590–1
118   C H Firth (ed), *Scotland and the Commonwealth* (SHS, 1895), 265
119   EDA, BL/3/1, Treasurer Receipt Book, 4 March 1661
120   Johnston, *Old Kirkintilloch*, 27–8
121   *ibid*, 29
122   *RPC*, 3rd ser, xv, 212
123   Horne, 'General expansion', 10–11
124   *Kirk Ct Bk*, 12, 20–1, 78–80, 137, 141
125   *ibid*, 135
126   *Glas Recs*, ii, 157
127   Johnston, *Old Kirkintilloch*, 32–3
128   *Kirk Ct Bk*, 74, 78, 103–4, 110, 135, 137
129   *NSA*, viii, 210
130   *NSA*, viii, 210
131   Watson, *Kirkintilloch*, 174; Martin, *Story of Kirkintilloch*, 22; Horne, 'General expansion', 21
132   *Kirk Ct Bk*, 108
133   *ibid*, 107
134   *ibid*, 128–9
135   For example *ibid*, 10, 19, 48, 72–3, 82, 103, 116, 128, 138
136   *The Commissariot Record of Glasgow: Register of Testaments, 1547–1800*, ed F J Grant (SRS, 1901), 142, 261, 456, 471, 491
137   A J Durie, *The Scottish Linen Industry in the Eighteenth Century* (Edinburgh, 1979), 88
138   *Kirk Ct Bk*, 6, 69, 108, 131, 126
139   Johnston, *Old Kirkintilloch*, 167
140   See for example *Kirk Ct Bk*, 3–4, 6–7, 121; EDA, GD85/1/11,13; Horne, 'General expansion', 11
141   *Kirk Ct Bk*, 35, 43, 63, 94–5, 105–6, 111, 120
142   *RMS*, xi, 238; *Kirk Ct Bk*, 5, 12, 48, 54, 56–7, 71, 104, 127, 139

143 F H Groome, *Ordnance Gazetteer of Scotland: A Survey of Scottish Topography, Statistical, Biographical, and Historical* (Edinburgh, 1883), v, 429

144 Martin, *Story of Kirkintilloch*, 23

145 *OSA*, ix, 77; R Heron, *Scotland Delineated* (Edinburgh, 1799), 210

146 Martin, *Story of Kirkintilloch*, 50; *Kirkintilloch's Past*, 8. It was by 1858 the Spade Forge Mill shown on the 1st Edition OS map

147 *OSA*, ix, 77–8

148 J Martin, 'Industrial advancement', in Horne, *Kirkintilloch*, 166

149 *NSA*, viii, 198–9; Martin, 'Industrial advancement', 166, 169; Martin, *Story of Kirkintilloch*, 50

150 *OSA*, ix, 78

151 *NSA*, viii, 194

152 Martin, 'Industrial advancement', 170–1

153 *NSA*, viii,198–9; Martin, 'Industrial advancement', 171; Martin, *Story of Kirkintilloch*, 50

154 Martin, 'Industrial advancement', 169; Martin, *Story of Kirkintilloch*, 50; S Selwyn and D Martin, *Kirkintilloch: Life and Times* (SDLM, 1994), 61

155 Hillis, *Country Town*, 52

156 Irvine, *Book of Dumbartonshire*, ii, 39

157 Martin, *Story of Kirkintilloch*, 52; Selwyn and Martin, *Kirkintilloch*, 61

158 Martin, 'Industrial advancement', 172–3; Selwyn and Martin, *Kirkintilloch*, 43

159 From the photo files relating to West High Street in the East Dunbartonshire Archives. We are indebted to Mr D Martin for his assistance on the location of the original tollhouse

160 *Kirkintilloch's Past*, 5–6

161 Watson, *Kirkintilloch*, 165; Martin, *Old Picture Postcards*, no. 3

162 Martin, 'Industrial advancement', 167

163 NAS, B66/25/498, Stirling Burgh Records

164 *NSA*, viii, 186; Watson, *Kirkintilloch*, 195

165 D Martin, *The Forth and Clyde Canal: A Kirkintilloch View* (SDLM, 2nd edn, 1985), 5

166 W Ferguson, *Scotland: 1689 to the Present* (Edinburgh, 1968), 195

167 Horne, 'General expansion', 18

168 Martin, *Forth and Clyde Canal*, 5

169 *Kirkintilloch's Past*, 8–9

170 Watson, *Kirkintilloch*, 168

171 D Loch, *A Tour through most of the Trading Towns and Villages of Scotland* (Edinburgh, 1778), 14

172 *NSA*, viii, 204

173 Martin, *Forth and Clyde Canal*, 19

174 Martin, 'Industrial advancement', 167

175 Martin, *Forth and Clyde Canal*, 24

176 A I Bowman, *Kirkintilloch Shipbuilding* (SDLM, 1983), 4

177 D Martin, *The Monkland and Kirkintilloch and Associated Railways* (SDLM, 1995), 5–6; Ferguson, *Scotland*, 295–6

178   Martin, *Kirkintilloch Railway*, 10

179   *ibid*, 11

180   Unless otherwise stated the information in the paragraph is based on
A I Bowman, *Kirkintilloch Shipbuilding* (SDLM, 1983)

181   Martin, 'Industrial advancement', 175; Martin, *Story of Kirkintilloch*, 53

182   Martin, 'Industrial advancement', 174–7; Martin, *Story of Kirkintilloch*, 53–5;
Selwyn and Martin, *Kirkintilloch*, 40

183   Martin, 'Industrial advancement', 185

184   *NSA*, viii, 199; Martin, 'Industrial advancement', 190–1

185   Selwyn and Martin, *Kirkintilloch*, 48

186   Martin, 'Industrial advancement', 182–3

187   Martin, *Story of Kirkintilloch*, 52–3

188   Martin, 'Industrial advancement', 182

189   Selwyn and Martin, *Kirkintilloch*, 54

190   Johnston, *Old Kirkintilloch*, 149–50

191   Selwyn and Martin, *Kirkintilloch*, 58; I H Adams, *The Making of Urban Scotland*
(London, 1978), 118

192   *NSA*, viii, 195

193   *ibid*, 210

194   Martin, 'Industrial advancement', 168

195   *NSA*, viii, 195–6

196   *ibid*, 210

197   Martin, 'Industrial advancement', 195–6

198   *OSA*, ix, 78

199   *NSA*, viii, 195

200   Martin, 'Industrial advancement', 170–1

210   Martin, *Story of Kirkintilloch*, 43

202   RCAHMS, *Tolbooths*, 127; Johnston, *Old Kirkintilloch*, 78–80

203   Martin, *Story of Kirkintilloch*, 34; Patrick, 'Burghal development', 73

204   Although the *New Statistical Account* is credited to Adam Forman, it was
probably drawn up by Rev William Patrick. We are indebted to Mr D Martin
for this information

205   *NSA*, viii, 205–6

206   Sunter, 'Ecclesiastical history', 110–11

207   Selwyn and Martin, *Kirkintilloch*, 10

208   Sunter, 'Ecclesiastical history', 119, 124, 131–3; Martin, *Story of Kirkintilloch*,
39–41; Martin, *Old Picture Postcards*, no. 52; Selwyn and Martin, *Kirkintilloch*,
13

209   Stewart, 'Schools and schoolmasters', 137–65; Martin, *Story of Kirkintilloch*,
36–8

210   Patrick, 'Burghal development', 42

211   R Handyside, 'Report on the Burgh of Barony of Kirkintilloch', *Reports of
Commissioners on Municipal Corporations, Scotland* (London, 1836), 109; Patrick,
'Burghal development', 42

212   Patrick, 'Burghal development', 52–3

213   Martin, *Story of Kirkintilloch*, 27–8

214 *ibid*, 30

215 Horne, 'General expansion', 23

216 Martin, *Story of Kirkintilloch*, 33

217 *ibid*, 31. In 1910 it was reported that while drains were being cut in the courtyard in Cowgate an old well was uncovered. It measured 14 ft in diameter by 12 ft deep and contained 18 in of water. The well was built of brick and coated with cement in a beehive form. It was calculated to be at least 100 years old and had been one of the main sources of water. It had been commonly known as Buchanan's Well. Horne, 'General expansion', 270

218 Watson, *Kirkintilloch*, 200–1

219 Horne, 'General expansion', 20–1

220 Watson, *Kirkintilloch*, 201

221 Martin, *Story of Kirkintilloch*, 31–2; J Shanks, *The Development of Public Services in Kirkintilloch 1870–1914* (Glasgow, 1980), 18–24

222 Patrick, 'Burghal development', 62

223 Martin, *Story of Kirkintilloch*, 32–3; Shanks, *Public Services*, 28

224 Horne, 'General expansion', 19

225 Hillis, *Country Town*, 70

226 Patrick, 'Burghal development', 62; Martin, *Story of Kirkintilloch*, 35–6

227 Shanks, *Public Services*, 13

228 Selwyn and Martin, *Kirkintilloch*, 59

229 Johnston, *Old Kirkintilloch*, 150

230 Hillis, *Country Town*, 33

231 Shanks, *Public Services*, 8

232 Watson, *Kirkintilloch*, 198

233 Patrick, 'Burghal development', 72–3

234 Watson, *Kirkintilloch*, 198–202; Hillis, *Country Town*; D Weir, *Kirkintilloch as it Existed Fifty Years Ago* (Glasgow, 1887)

235 A Fullarton, *The Topographical, Statistical, and Historical Gazetteer of Scotland* (Glasgow, 1842), ii, 181

236 For example, J P Lawson, *An Enlarged Gazetteer of Scotland* (Edinburgh, 1841), 730; Groome, *Ordnance Gazetteer*, iv, 428

237 Fletcher, 'Burgh and parish', 289; *Johnston's Gazetteer of Scotland*, revised by R W Munro (London, 3rd edn, 1973), 213

238 Martin, *Forth and Clyde Canal*, 29–30; *Kirkintilloch's Past*, 10

239 Selwyn and Martin, *Kirkintilloch*, 54

240 *ibid*, 43; Fletcher, 'Burgh and parish', 298

241 Bowman, *Shipbuilding*, 55

242 Selwyn and Martin, *Kirkintilloch*, 44

243 Bowman, *Shipbuilding*, 43–4, 55

244 Martin, *Story of Kirkintilloch*, 56–7; Kirkintilloch WEA Retirement Class, *Two Communities: Springburn and Kirkintilloch: A Chronicle of Glasgow Overspill* (SDLM, 1983), 28–9

245 Fletcher, 'Burgh and parish', 294

246 Selwyn and Martin, *Kirkintilloch*, 59

247   *ibid*, 5
248   Fletcher, 'Burgh and parish', 292
249   *The Burgh of Kirkintilloch: the Official Guide* (London, nd), 11
250   Selwyn and Martin, *Kirkintilloch*, 58

4 Area by area assessment

Area 1: Peel Park

Sites and locations mentioned in this area are shown in **figure 29**.

Roman fort and the Antonine Wall

Several archaeological excavations undertaken within Peel Park have shown that this was the location of a Roman fort (**fig 22**). The area has been designated a Scheduled Ancient Monument in order to protect the archaeological remains which survive beneath the surface of the park. It forms a link in the Frontiers of the Roman Empire World Heritage Site that was inscribed by UNESCO in 2005, to which the Antonine Wall was added in 2008.

The excavations roughly defined the area of the fort, having uncovered the outer ditches in several places (**figs 22 & 23**). Some remains relating to its interior features have also been recorded. It should be pointed out, however, that the excavations generally involved only small trenches and the fort's layout remains poorly understood. Some indirect evidence has been interpreted as suggesting that there may have been an annexe possibly containing a bath-house to the south and east of the fort.[1] Many finds have been recovered during the excavations, notably fragments of glass vessels, amphorae, Samian drinking vessels and tiles.[2] The basal fills of the ditches have been found to be waterlogged as can be seen in **figure 23**.[3] Waterlogging is beneficial to the archaeological resource as rare organic materials such as wood and leather may be preserved; in this case Roman sandals were recovered.[4]

It is thought that in common with many others on the Antonine Wall the fort was deliberately slighted during the Romans' withdrawal. Certainly some of the excavations have suggested that Roman masonry from the bath house was thrown into the ditch.[5] Reused stone in surrounding walls and buildings, identified by distinctive cross-hatching scored onto the stone surface of parts of the Auld Kirk, may then be Roman or medieval.

In addition to remains relating to the fort, the line of the Wall has been confirmed within Peel Park (**fig 22**). This differs slightly from that depicted by the Ordnance Survey, shown on **figure 29.6**.[6] To the east and west it disappears below the modern town and there is some uncertainty as to its exact course. Based on negative and equivocal results, however, it is thought to have run to the north or under the Auld Kirk, rather than to the south as shown in **figure 29**, and possibly around 50m south of High Street on the line of the relief road (New Lairdsland Road).[7] Further east its line has been

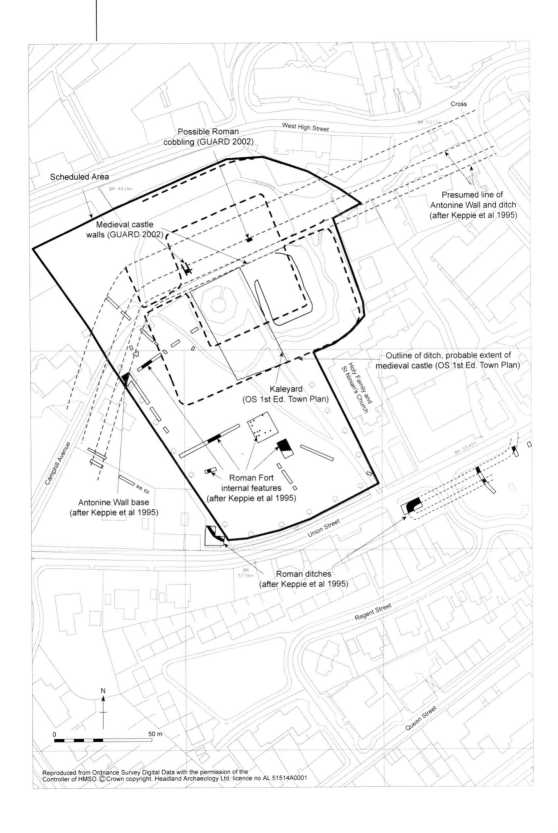

Cross

West High Street

Possible Roman
cobbling (GUARD 2002)

Scheduled Area

BM 44.14m

Presumed line of
Antonine Wall and ditch
(after Keppie et al 1995)

Medieval castle
walls (GUARD 2002)

Outline of ditch, probable extent of
medieval castle (OS 1st Ed. Town Plan)

Holy Family and
St Ninian's Church

Kaleyard
(OS 1st Ed. Town Plan)

BM 55.49m

Roman Fort
internal features
(after Keppie et al 1995)

Camphill Avenue

Antonine Wall base
(after Keppie et al 1995)

Union Street

BM
57.56m

Roman ditches
(after Keppie et al 1995)

Regent Street

N

0   50 m

Quean Street

Reproduced from Ordnance Survey Digital Data with the permission of the
Controller of HMSO. © Crown copyright. Headland Archaeology Ltd. licence no AL 51514A0001

confirmed by excavation in two places to the north of Hillhead Road (**fig 29.36 & 37**).[8]

Medieval castle

It is assumed that the Peel, normally taken to refer to a wooden defensive palisade, which formerly occupied Peel Park (**fig 29.1**), is synonymous with the Castle of Kirkintilloch built by the Comyns in the twelfth or thirteenth century.[9] It seems very likely that the name 'Peel' derives from the wooden palisade built or rebuilt around the castle site by the English in 1302.[10] As it stands today, the Peel appears to be a small earthen mound with a ditch defining it to the east and south. It is known from documents, however, that the part of the castle to the west of this mound was levelled to form a

FIGURE 23:
Union Street excavations, showing Roman ditch under excavation by R D Stevenson in 1978–79 (By courtesy of East Dunbartonshire Information and Archives)

kaleyard in the 1830s (**fig 22**).[11] The first edition Ordnance Survey town plans (surveyed 1859) appear to show the kaleyard accurately and also the outline of the ditch of the castle, although it is erroneously identified as a 'Roman Wall Station'.[12] This is shown overlaid on the modern plan in **figure 22.** The ditch forms a simple square shape, with internal dimensions measuring roughly 60m². The form as depicted in early maps does not seem to represent a typical motte and bailey castle; instead it has far more in common with early stone castles, which comprised simple square ditched enclosures with an internal curtain wall. A very similar example, in terms of form, dimensions and date, is Auchen Castle in Annandale.[13] The appearance of the Peel today, an earthen mound suggesting an origin as a motte, seems likely to be a result of landscaping starting with the formation of the kaleyard in the 1830s. Excavations undertaken within this area in 2002 as part of landscaping works uncovered the remains of substantial stone wall foundations (**fig 22**), some of which may have formed part of a vaulted structure.[14] Presumably the square enclosure contained a courtyard defended by a massive curtain wall and containing many stone buildings and wells. An excavation was undertaken on the site of the castle in 1899, as summarised by Stevenson in 1979, and apparently uncovered thick stone walls possibly relating to a keep and an outer courtyard wall. Unfortunately the exact location of these was never recorded.[15]

It should be noted that medieval finds, and possibly a medieval stone drain, have been found further south in the park, outside the area defined by the ditch.[16] The rough outline of the Roman fort seems to have persisted as property boundaries up to the modern period, suggesting they remained visible in some form throughout the medieval occupation of the site. It is possible that the remainder of the park, to the south of the central enclosure, was used as an outer annexe of the castle and perhaps housed ancillary buildings, although this is speculative. The finds of stone capitals or pillars to the east of the castle, noted previously, suggest that a chapel may have been associated with it as early as the thirteenth century. This may be synonymous with a chapel dedicated to the Virgin Mary documented in the fourteenth century. The foundations of the Auld Kirk seem to lie on top of earlier ones, and the site may have been the location for a chapel associated with the castle and lying just outside its entrance at the top of Peel Brae.

Later history

The Auld Kirk (**fig 29.3**), a listed building, was built in 1644, as inscribed on its date stone located above a window in the south gable. It seems to have been altered from early in its history, with later changes to some doors and windows.[17] More extensive alterations were carried out in the late eighteenth century when galleries were inserted and forestairs constructed to access them.[18] Some lesser alterations were carried out in the nineteenth century, and it was converted to its current use as a museum in 1961, but has subsequently been improved at various dates, most notably in 2001. Inside, some of the eighteenth-century woodwork survives as galleries and a pulpit, as well as a bell dated to 1663. Several of the gravestones in the churchyard date to the eighteenth century.

A Roman Catholic school and chapel were built in the south-eastern part of the former Roman fort in 1875.[19] This building was extended and used as a hall following construction of the Holy Family and St Ninian church between 1891 and 1893. Both are listed buildings (**fig 29.34**).[20] Peel Park was laid out in 1898, with the listed bandstand and fountain, both made by the Lion Foundry in 1905 (**figs 19 & 29.29**), and the war memorial (**fig 29.38**) in 1925.[21] Archaeological excavations have shown that the southern edge of the park was the site of air raid shelters in the Second World War, and these have removed all earlier archaeological remains.[22]

Area 2: High Street and Eastside

The medieval burgh

Historical records show that there was a burgh associated with the castle as early as 1211.[23] The extent and location of this settlement is not clear from historical records, but it is known that it had a weekly market. Certainly as depicted by Roy *c* 1750 (**fig 4**), the town's pre-modern location appears to be on an east–west axis along High Street and Eastside. Properties in medieval burghs take the standard form of plots or rigs, thin strips of land stretching at right angles from the main street. These can clearly be seen surviving to the north of The Cross on the first edition Ordnance Survey plans of the town (**figs 24 & 29.7**). Their layout is very irregular in both shape and size, as well as how far into the street the frontage buildings extend. In part this suggests that the road was primary, originating as a major routeway from Glasgow to the east and north-east, and predated the development of the burgh. The rather haphazard angles the plots were forced to adopt reflect the need to fit in with the surrounding topography while maintaining a parallel frontage with the street. Generally the plots vary in width from 6m to 10m, comfortably within the range expected in medieval towns. Often it is possible to establish the sequence of development of a town because plots laid out at the same time tend to be the same width. This does not seem to be possible in Kirkintilloch, with little sign of a regular sequence of development. What is very noticeable is that the plots to the north of The Cross are much more densely occupied than those elsewhere in the town. They contain many more buildings set back from the street, with closes to provide access to them. One of these closes survives between nos 16 and 20 High Street (**figs 25 & 29.13**).

Oxgang and Waterside (fig 24, insets 3 & 4)

As noted in the previous section, the parish church of the medieval town was St Ninian's at Oxgang (fig 1). The former area of the church lies within the Old Aisle or Auld Isle burial ground and is now wooded; the ground level is some 2m higher than the surrounding modern cemetery. The entrance to it is through a gateway (see fig 6), possibly dating to the early eighteenth century, and perhaps used in the early nineteenth as a watch house against 'resurrectionists'. The standing gravestones date mainly to the nineteenth century, although some late eighteenth-century ones can be identified. A large fragment of stone sculpture, which has not been securely dated but seems most likely to date to the medieval or post-medieval period, was found in the churchyard around 1915.[24] The sculpture seems to depict some sort of animal, although interpretations have varied.

It is also possible that Oxgang was the site of the town's mill, as an 'Old Mill' is marked here on the first edition Ordnance Survey map (fig 24, inset 3; location north of Oxgang on fig 1), on the north bank east of the roundabout. A second ruined mill is shown slightly further away on the Luggie Water at Duntiblae, Waterside, with a distillery, gas works, Subscription School and Spade Forge Mill, believed to have been the lint mill of 1777.[25] An old photograph in East Dunbartonshire Information and Archives shows that the latter had steep crow-stepped gables and a wheel with timber spokes at its gable. These sites have archaeological potential.[26]

The Cross got its name because this is the former location of the market cross; as noted in the previous section, this was destroyed by vandals in 1815. The lack of recognisably medieval plots on the south side of High Street here, and the location outside the entrance to the castle, all lend credence to the suggestion that this was where the weekly market was held. This would help to explain why the plots to the north were the most developed, as a location next to the market would be the most attractive for commercial purposes. There was certainly a concentration of inns here in the nineteenth century, as would be expected around a market place.[27]

Several archaeological excavations concentrating on the town rather than the fort and castle have been undertaken since the 1970s.[28] Five areas in total have been subject to archaeological trenching. No archaeological deposits were seen in a trench in the front garden of no. 17 Regent Street (fig 29.39) or during trenching in advance of the creation of the Regent Street car park (fig 29.40). Excavation at a site on Union Street uncovered evidence of the Roman fort and has been discussed above. Two neighbouring sites on East High Street (fig 29.41 & 42) both produced medieval pottery, but only one contained surviving archaeological features. Trenching here (fig 29.41) established that modern building had removed any archaeological remains on the street frontage; to the rear, however, a number of medieval features including a cobbled yard, drains, rubbish pits and a possible cess-pit were recorded.[29] Large unabraded sherds of pottery, thought to date between the twelfth and fifteenth centuries, were recovered, and suggested that little

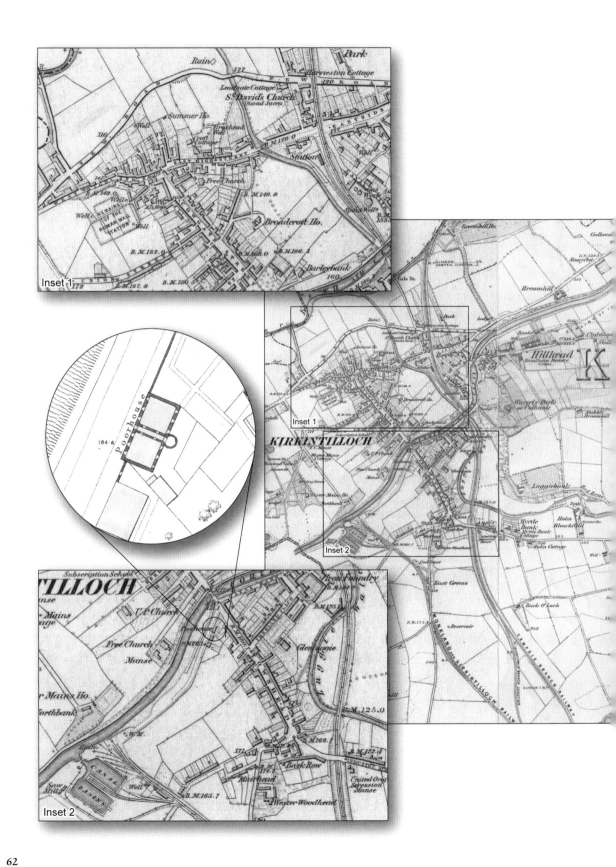

Inset 1

Inset 2

Poorhouse

KIRKINTILLOCH

Inset 1

Inset 2

1st edition Ordnance Survey map of Kirkintilloch, published in 1864 (Reproduced by
permission of the Trustees of the National Library of Scotland)
Inset 1, detail of High Street and Cowgate
Inset 2, detail of Townhead
Inset 3, detail of Oxgang
Inset 4, detail of Waterside

disturbance had occurred. One of these sherds was thought to be a fragment of imported German stoneware.

Near The Cross, on the north side of High Street, an excavation undertaken between 1987 and 1988 established that this area has been heavily disturbed (**fig 29.43**).[30] Medieval pottery was recovered from a possible beam slot, suggesting that timber buildings may once have occupied the area.

A stone-lined well, possibly of medieval date, was recorded during excavation work for the relief road (New Lairdsland Road).[31] Many such wells must have existed in the backlands of medieval properties.

Taken together these excavations confirm that High Street, from The Cross at least as far as the area shown in **figure 29.42**, had been developed in the medieval period. Rather more tentatively, the possible structural remains from the excavation beside The Cross suggest that building in the backlands had begun in the medieval period, supporting the suggestion that this was traditionally the most developed area of the town.

FIGURE 25:
Close at no. 18 High Street with Barony Chambers in the background, 2004

Post-medieval development

It is known from documents that a ruinous bridge existed over the Luggie Water in 1598, but it is not known when this was erected.[32] A stone bridge was constructed in 1672 and rebuilt in 1727 (*see* **fig 13**).[33] The Luggie Bridge was entirely renewed during the 1790s. This presumably is the bridge that still stands (**fig 29.9**), with some later additions of ironwork, and it has been protected as a listed building (Category B-listed).

The Barony Chambers (Category B-listed) (*see* **figs 21 & 29.11**) were constructed in the early nineteenth century as a replacement for the burgh's tolbooth, which had stood on the site from at least the seventeenth century.[34]

A greater number of documents survive from the seventeenth century and it is clear that by this date, if not considerably earlier, Eastside existed and the town had spread across the Luggie Water. As shown on Roy's map of *c* 1750 (*see* **fig 4**), development seems to have been limited on the north-west side of town, presumably due to the steep slope. West High Street contains the farm of Westermains (Category B-listed) (*see* **figs 7 & 29.12**), a short terrace of early nineteenth-century, or possibly earlier, cottages, which would originally have been thatched.[35] While 'Mains' means estate farm, it would have been cut off from any fields by the new Glasgow Road. There is a small octagonal summerhouse or watch house on the north boundary and at the foot of the slope on the north side of Glasgow Road is a nineteenth-century tollhouse (Category B-listed) (*see* **figs 17 & 29.17**).

Some sources state that throughout the area of the medieval town, surviving vernacular buildings date from *c* 1800 at the earliest.[36] It is vital, however, that the dating of the early buildings of Kirkintilloch is re-examined (*see* documentary source potential, p 77). The older buildings have three concentrations, one being the Westermains farm buildings and another the area to the north of The Cross at nos 16–22 High Street (**fig 29.13**). The third group of buildings lies on Eastside (**fig 29.16**), where modern development has been less intensive. These buildings may contain features relating to their earlier uses, such as blocked windows and fireplaces.

Area 3: Cowgate and Townhead (fig 24, insets 1 & 2)

Medieval route

It is clear from Roy's map that Cowgate was not the main thoroughfare of the medieval town, and had not been built up by the mid-eighteenth century, a fact confirmed by excavations undertaken in the area. Some later features were discovered during the excavations, in addition to the southern edge of the Roman fort.[37] Although no dating evidence was recovered from these, their stratigraphic position suggested they were of relatively late date. More firm dating evidence was provided by a trial excavation (**fig 29.44**), which recovered some late medieval pottery, probably derived from manuring fields around the town, as well as late post-medieval features.[38] The roadway itself presumably had a medieval origin, leading south to Townhead and then to Oxgang. As suggested in the previous section, it probably operated as a local thoroughfare, in contrast to the important route along High Street, and hence it was less attractive for medieval development.

Roy's map does depict some settlement at Townhead by the eighteenth century (*see* **fig 4**), while historical documents suggest that this area had sustained at least some development by the middle of the seventeenth century; this could presumably have been medieval in origin.[39]

Industrial development

Following the opening of this section of the Forth and Clyde Canal in 1773, the focus of the town changed and Cowgate began to replace High Street as the main thoroughfare. Development seems to have been rapid and both Cowgate and its continuation, Townhead, had been intensively developed by the mid-nineteenth century (**fig 24**).[40] Development had also occurred on both sides of the canal at Hillhead by this time.[41]

The canal and related feeder channel are designated as a Scheduled Ancient Monument (**fig 29.4**). The canal runs in an aqueduct over the Luggie Water (**fig 29.5**). At Hillhead it is crossed by a steel wing bridge dated 1938 (**fig 29.45**), [42] which replaced an earlier bascule bridge. The original wooden bascule bridge at Townhead was replaced in 1933 (**figs 26 & 29.21**).[43] Associated structures were to be found along the length of the canal, such as at Glasgow Bridge to the west of town where an old stable still stands (**fig 1**).

Other sites intimately associated with the canal were its harbours and shipyards, of which there were three in the town. The harbour or Hillhead Basin (**fig 29.19**) was the first inland harbour on a man-made waterway in Scotland. Two dockyards were situated on the canal to the south-east. From 1835 the Kirkintilloch Basin (**fig 29.24**) served as the terminus for the Monkland to Kirkintilloch Railway, with coal transferred to waiting ships. The railway and canal basins can be seen on **figure 24**.[44] A shipyard was developed there in 1902, while to the north a yard operated by J and J Hay (**fig 29.4**) was operational from the 1860s.[45] Some evidence of these yards can still be seen by the side of the canal, the most substantial surviving remains being the Hays' repair slip (**fig 29.23**), opened in 1889, which is set away from the boat-building yard. The original canal basin lies outwith the scheduled monument as it was filled in before scheduling. It has been excavated as part of the mitigation strategy for construction of a boathouse, as a condition of planning permission.[46]

Of the other industries that sprung up in the town following the opening of the canal, one of the most important was iron founding. The Old Foundry

FIGURE 26:
Townhead and the bascule
bridge over the Forth
and Clyde Canal, c 1905
(By courtesy of East
Dunbartonshire Information
and Archives)

FIGURE 27:
2nd edition Ordnance Survey
map of Stirlingshire sheet
XXXII.NW, surveyed in
1898 and published in 1899
(Reproduced by permission
of the Trustees of the
National Library of Scotland)

(fig 29.25) was operating in the mid-nineteenth century and its layout can be seen in figure 24.[47] Two more foundries, the Star Foundry and the Basin Foundry (fig 29.26 & 27), were opened shortly afterwards but the most famous establishment was the Lion Foundry (fig 29.28), set up c 1880, which specialised in decorative ironwork. All the foundries are visible on figure 27.[48] As part of this industrial expansion a gasworks had been constructed in the town by 1866 (figs 27 & 29.35).[49] All of these industrial complexes have since closed.

Much of the Cowgate has been redeveloped in the twentieth century, but one group of mixed older buildings survives at nos 93–129 Cowgate (fig 29.46). The dating of Kirkintilloch's older buildings could usefully be re-examined (*see* documentary source potential).

Notes

1   L J F Keppie, G B Bailey, A J Dunwell, J H McBrien and K Speller, 'Some excavations on the line of the Antonine Wall 1985–93' *Proc Soc Antiq Scot*, cxxv (1995), 653

2   A S Robertson, 'Miscellanea Romano-Caledonica' *Proc Soc Antiq Scot*, xcvii (1963–64), 180–8

3   R D Stevenson, *Kirkintilloch: Trial Trenching 1978–79* (Glasgow Archaeological Society Bulletin, New Series, No. 9, Spring 1980)

4   *ibid*

5   Keppie *et al*, 'Some excavations', 653

6   Robertson, 'Miscellanea Romano-Caledonica', 188

7   *ibid*, 180; Keppie *et al*, 'Some excavations', 649

8   J A Atkinson, 'The Manse, Hillhead Road', *DES* (1994), 80; K Speller, 'St Flannan's Church, Antonine Wall', *DES* (1995), 92

9   This volume, p 15

10   D Martin, *Kirkintilloch Castle* (East Dunbartonshire Archives, 2003), *passim*

11   This volume, p 59

12   Ordnance Survey first edition, 1866 *Kirkintilloch Town Plan*, Dunbartonshire sheet xxiv 8.19, 1:500

13   RCAHMS, *Eastern Dumfriesshire an archaeological landscape* (Edinburgh, 1977), 202

14   D Swan and H James, Peel Park, Kirkintilloch (unpublished GUARD client report, 2003)

15   R D Stevenson, Interim Report on Archaeological Excavations in Kirkintilloch, 1978–79 (unpublished archive report).

16   *ibid;* Robertson 'Miscellanea Romano-Caledonica', 180–8

17   J Gifford and F A Walker, *The Buildings of Scotland: Stirling and Central Scotland* (London, 2002), 567

18   *ibid*, 568

19   *ibid*, 573

20   *ibid*, 567

21 *ibid*, 572

22 Robertson, 'Miscellanea Romano-Caledonica', 186

23 This volume, p 13

24 J Fletcher, 'Two Kirkintilloch Antiquities: carved dragon head and short cist', *Proc Soc Antiq Scot*, lxxxvi (1951–52), 202

25 Ordnance Survey, first edition surveyed 1858, published 1864–65, Dumbartonshire sheet xxv

26 East Dumbartonshire Online/ local history pictures/ ecards online http://www.eastdunbarton.gov.uk/web%20site/live/visiting/Virtual%20Postcards.nsf/WebImageGallery?OpenForm&Category=Local%20History

27 Ordnance Survey first edition, 1866 *Kirkintilloch Town Plan*, Dunbartonshire sheet xxiv 8.19, 1:500

28 Stevenson, *Interim Report*

29 *ibid*

30 L Casebow, Excavations at Salford Place, Kirkintilloch 1987–88: Interim Report (unpublished SUAT archive report)

31 Keppie *et al*, 'Some excavations', 649

32 See this volume, p 25

33 *ibid*

34 This volume, p 41

35 Gifford and Walker, *Buildings of Scotland*, 574

36 *ibid*, 575

37 Keppie *et al*, 'Some excavations', 652

38 P Holdsworth, 'Kirkintilloch: Cowgate', *DES* (1986), 39

39 This volume, pp 18–19

40 Ordnance Survey, first edition, 1866 *Kirkintilloch Town Plan*, Dumbartonshire sheet xxiv 8.19 & 25, 1:500

41 Ordnance Survey, first edition, 1866 *Kirkintilloch Town Plan*, Dumbartonshire sheet xxiv 8.15 & 20, 1:500

42 NMRS, Record NS67SE 68

43 *ibid*, 46

44 *ibid*, 70

45 This volume, pp 37

46 Information from Historic Scotland

47 J R Hume, *The Industrial Archaeology of Scotland, 1: The Lowlands and Borders* (London 1976), 111; Ordnance Survey, first edition, 1866 *Kirkintilloch Town Plan*, Dumbartonshire sheet xxiv 8.25, 1:500

48 Hume, *Industrial Archaeology*, 111

49 Ordnance Survey, first edition, 1866 *Kirkintilloch Town Plan*, Dumbartonshire sheet xxiv 8.20, 1:500

5 The potential of Kirkintilloch

See **figure 28**.

Archaeological potential

Area 1: Peel Park

The archaeological potential of this part of the town is well established. It is known to contain internationally important remains relating to the Antonine Wall, that is now inscribed as a World Heritage Site. One of the most important aspects of recent archaeological investigations has been the identification of the medieval castle, which overlies the fort, as a possibly much earlier stone castle than previously thought. These archaeological remains have the potential to increase substantially our knowledge concerning the development of castles in Scotland. The area has been designated a Scheduled Ancient Monument in order to protect these Roman and medieval remains but excavations have shown that the edges of the Roman fort extend beyond the Scheduled Area. This larger area is shown as dark green in **figure 28**. Also outside the Scheduled Area, the Auld Kirk may well occupy the site of a medieval chapel associated with the castle.

Area 2: High Street and Eastside

Medieval Kirkintilloch developed around High Street and Eastside, and consequently this area has a high potential to contain important archaeological remains.

The area of High Street around The Cross has seen a substantial amount of development over the last twenty years, but archaeological excavations have established that medieval remains may be preserved in the area, especially in backlands where post-medieval and modern development has not been so intensive. With regard to large-scale modern developments, such as the William Patrick Library (**fig 29.2**), it is not easy to predict whether these will have removed all traces of earlier remains, although with developments of this kind it seems likely. The archaeological potential of areas beneath these buildings is lower than undeveloped areas, but, depending on the foundation techniques and whether the site was cleared before construction began, there is a possibility that some pockets of archaeology may survive. The pre-twentieth-century structures surviving around The Cross, notably between nos 16 and 20 High Street (**fig 29.13**), have the potential to contain within their fabric information relating to their development and uses. It is likely that

FIGURE 28:
(opposite) Archaeological potential of Kirkintilloch

FIGURE 29:
(pages 72–3) Locations and sites mentioned in the text

World Heritage Site
Rest of medieval town
Post-medieval and industrial expansion
N
0
250 m
© Crown Copyright

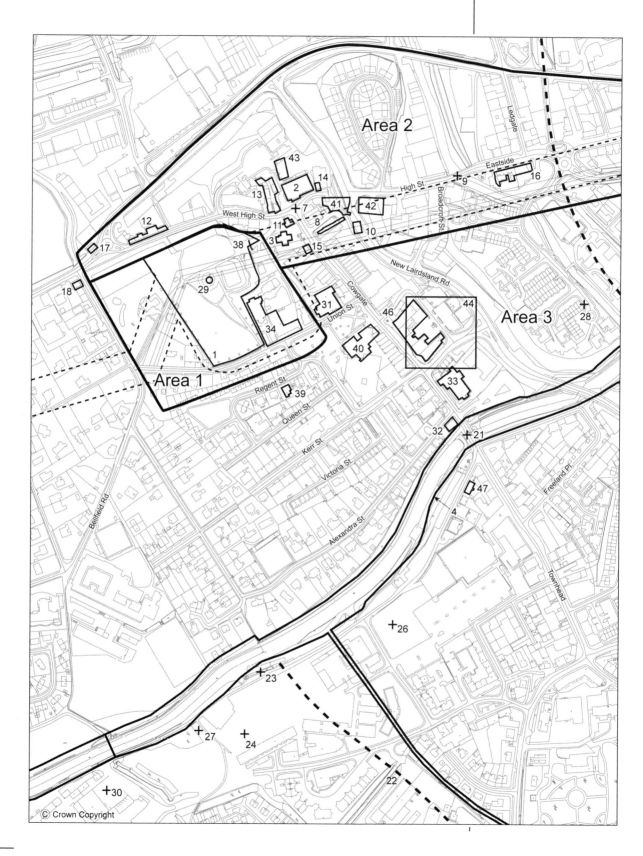

Area 2

Area 1

Area 3

Ledgate

Eastside

High St.

West High St.

Broadcroft St.

New Lairdsland Rd.

Cowgate

Union St.

Regent St.

Queen St.

Kerr St.

Victoria St.

Alexandra St.

Bellfield Rd.

Freeland Pl.

Townhead

© Crown Copyright

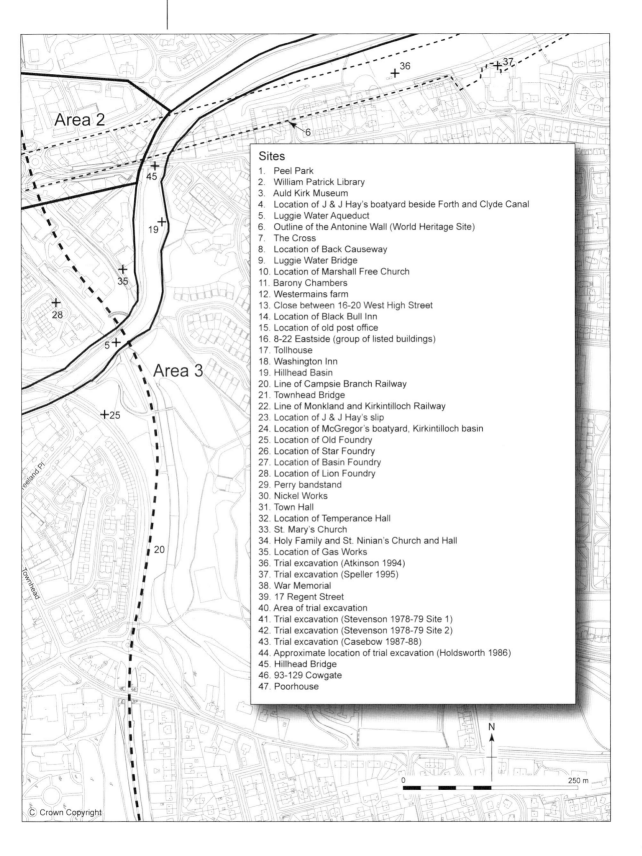

Sites

1. Peel Park
2. William Patrick Library
3. Auld Kirk Museum
4. Location of J & J Hay's boatyard beside Forth and Clyde Canal
5. Luggie Water Aqueduct
6. Outline of the Antonine Wall (World Heritage Site)
7. The Cross
8. Location of Back Causeway
9. Luggie Water Bridge
10. Location of Marshall Free Church
11. Barony Chambers
12. Westermains farm
13. Close between 16-20 West High Street
14. Location of Black Bull Inn
15. Location of old post office
16. 8-22 Eastside (group of listed buildings)
17. Tollhouse
18. Washington Inn
19. Hillhead Basin
20. Line of Campsie Branch Railway
21. Townhead Bridge
22. Line of Monkland and Kirkintilloch Railway
23. Location of J & J Hay's slip
24. Location of McGregor's boatyard, Kirkintilloch basin
25. Location of Old Foundry
26. Location of Star Foundry
27. Location of Basin Foundry
28. Location of Lion Foundry
29. Perry bandstand
30. Nickel Works
31. Town Hall
32. Location of Temperance Hall
33. St. Mary's Church
34. Holy Family and St. Ninian's Church and Hall
35. Location of Gas Works
36. Trial excavation (Atkinson 1994)
37. Trial excavation (Speller 1995)
38. War Memorial
39. 17 Regent Street
40. Area of trial excavation
41. Trial excavation (Stevenson 1978-79 Site 1)
42. Trial excavation (Stevenson 1978-79 Site 2)
43. Trial excavation (Casebow 1987-88)
44. Approximate location of trial excavation (Holdsworth 1986)
45. Hillhead Bridge
46. 93-129 Cowgate
47. Poorhouse

N

0   250 m

sub-surface archaeological remains survive at least in places beneath these older structures.

The relief road that divides High Street runs in a deep cutting into the natural slope. It is inevitable that this will have removed any archaeological features that once existed within its corridor. To the east of the road, development has been less intensive than around The Cross. Although many modern buildings exist in the area, these are mainly single-storey industrial blocks which may not have extensive or deep foundations. Open land such as car parks also occupy substantial portions of the area. It seems likely that at least in places archaeological remains may be preserved. The potential survival of deeply cut archaeological features, such as the Antonine ditch and wells, is high. On the north side of the road, the residential development around Braehead Street is likely to have damaged many archaeological deposits when it was constructed in the early part of the twentieth century, although again some areas, especially between buildings, may contain surviving pockets of archaeological remains.

Eastside has not seen extensive modern development. It is not known when this part of the town first developed and only archaeological excavation can resolve this issue. The archaeological potential of this part of town has not been tested, but it seems likely that, at least in places, some archaeological remains relating to medieval or post-medieval development survive. Some buildings possibly dating from as early as the late eighteenth century, and certainly the nineteenth century, survive in the town and they have the potential to contain information about their earlier uses preserved within their fabric.

Area 3: Cowgate and Townhead

Cowgate, although perhaps with a genesis as a medieval route, is thought to have been developed largely as part of the town's expansion following the opening of the Forth and Clyde Canal. Some areas, such as Townhead, may have developed in the medieval period. Modern development has been extensive on and around the street.

This area does contain important visible remains relating to industrial archaeology. Paramount among these is the canal itself, and associated structures, protected by designation as a Scheduled Ancient Monument. Elsewhere, remains relating to post-medieval development and industrial sites, for example the town's foundries, may survive as sub-surface remains where not disturbed by modern development. Remains relating to both dockyards (**fig 29.23 & 24**) seem likely to survive in some form outside the Scheduled Area of the canal. Where it is clear that cellars or basements have been excavated, such as at no. 17 High Street (**fig 29.41**), no remains will survive.

Few buildings earlier than the twentieth century survive on Cowgate, the major exception being nos 93–129 Cowgate, a block of mixed date (**fig 29.46**). These buildings, although dating to the later eighteenth century at the earliest, and more probably the nineteenth century, may contain original features. The recording of these, and of similar buildings in Townhead, like the poorhouse in Southbank Road (**fig 30**) (did it operate a weaving shop for inmates on the ground floor, as the layout given in the OS 1st Edition 1:500 Town Plan suggests?), could add to our knowledge of the town's history in the industrial period.

FIGURE 30:
The poorhouse on Southbank Road. The OS 1:500 Town Plan (surveyed in 1858) shows the central pend leading to a spiral stair (see fig 24, inset 2). The other two doors are later insertions in place of windows, so the arrangement was very similar to loom shops in the town, perhaps here also with a cellar loom shop, to keep inmates gainfully employed

Handloom shops

Standing buildings archaeology notes the way that building fabric can illuminate changes in economy and in society. The handloom shop is a building type evident in old photographs of Kirkintilloch. Records of the Dean of Guild capture the conversion of several of these to full residential use in around 1890,[1] and at least two examples survive: in Union Street and in Townhead ('Wagtail', Muirhead Street). These early nineteenth-century buildings comprised first-floor tenement housing reached by a pend and a rear turnpike stair. The pend split the ground floor into two compartments of unequal size, and access to these was obtained from the pend rather than the street. Ground-floor windows were smaller than those above, and almost square (still evident at no. 7 Muirhead Street in Townhead). The absence of a door to the street, and the small size of the windows, helped to maintain a moist climate to prevent breakage of the warp yarn. Windows would have lit a loom each, so around ten looms would have been worked in what were clearly small factories. This counters the traditional image of the independent weaver outworking in his own cottage. Factory organisation is a characteristic of handloom shops in Scotland.[2] Evidently cotton weaving persisted in Kirkintilloch in handloom shops (**figs 31 & 32**), as well as in a few powerloom factories.

FIGURE 31:
One of the last handloom weavers in Kirkintilloch, weaving two widths of cloth at once on a broadloom placed on an earthen floor, side on to natural light with windows positioned above the working area of the loom (By courtesy of East Dunbartonshire Information and Archives)

FIGURE 32:
A handloom shop with square ground-floor windows and high sills to suit similar looms, adapted to dwellings as Martin's Land, Broadcroft, before its demolition in 1959 (By courtesy of East Dunbartonshire Information and Archives)

Documentary source potential

There are few documentary materials relating to Kirkintilloch prior to 1600, and this will inhibit further research. There is significantly more material for the seventeenth and eighteenth centuries, and it may be possible to begin to reconstruct the community in this period through the use of the Burgh Court Books, Treasurer's Accounts, Kirk Session records, sasines and testaments. This could provide a valuable insight into the small-scale semi-agrarian community prior to its transformation in the nineteenth century. From the nineteenth century the available sources are extensive. These have been used in a number of studies, but it is felt there is still more to learn about the burgh during a period of major change.

It is important that the dating of Kirkintilloch's early buildings is re-examined. Local knowledge is at variance with some of the dating suggested by Gifford and Walker (2002). Correct dating through historical and archaeological analysis is the key to any attempt to provide an overview of the architectural development of Kirkintilloch.

Notes

1   East Dunbartonshire archives. Reproduced in S Selwyn and D Martin, *Kirkintilloch Life and Times* (1994), pp 60–1
2   See for example E P Dennison *et al*, *Historic Galashiels* (forthcoming)

Glossary of technical terms

Anglo-Saxons	people who settled in Britain from the Low Countries and Germany in the fifth or sixth centuries; also described as Angles
artefacts	anything modified or made by people, including pottery, objects made from bone, wood or metal, carved stone etc
backlands	the area to the rear of the burgage plot behind the dwelling house on the frontage, originally intended for growing produce and keeping animals in addition to being the site of wells and midden heaps. Eventually housed working premises of craftsmen and poorer members of the burgh society
bailies	burgh officers who preformed routine administration
beam slot	the foundation trench for a timber building
Bronze Age	the prehistoric period between the Neolithic (*qv*) and the Iron Age (*qv*) or *c* 2000–500 BC in Scotland, so named because of the introduction of bronze working
burgage plot	a division of land, often regular in size, having been measured out by liners, allocated to a burgess. Once built on, it contained the burgage house on the frontage (*qv*) and a backland (*qv*). Over time, with pressure for space, the plots were often subdivided. Plots were bounded by ditches, wattle fences or stone walls
burgess	a person who enjoyed the privileges and responsibilities of the freedom of the burgh
Canmore	a computerised database maintained by RCAHMS which covers the whole of Scotland and contains information on many standing buildings, chance finds and archaeological works
casualties	casual or incidental charges or sources of income
close	alley or narrow lane
cooper	a maker of casks and barrels
cordiner	leather worker, usually a shoe maker
conservation area	area of special architectural or historic interest, the character or appearance of which it is desirable to preserve or enhance, under the terms of the Planning (Listed Buildings and Conservation Areas) (Scotland) Act 1997

cropmarks	a means through which sub-surface archaeological, natural and recent features may be visible from the air or a vantage point on higher ground. They can reveal buried archaeological sites not visible from the ground. Cropmarks appear due to the principle of differential growth; for example, a buried wall will cause the ground above to be drier and plants will ripen more quickly, forming a line with a slightly different colour
crow-stepped gables	step-like projections up the sloping edge of a gable
curtain wall	a wall placed around a castle
Dark Ages	The period between the collapse of the western Roman Empire and the establishment of the feudal medieval system, c AD 400–1000
documentary sources	written evidence, primary sources being the original documents
evaluation	a programme of site investigations often comprising desk-based research and trial trenching
excavation	the controlled removal and recording of archaeological deposits, often following an evaluation (qv) which has established their presence
feu	a perpetual lease at a fixed rent
finds	a term used to refer to artefacts but also including environmental remains such as seeds and bones
flax dresser	hackler or heckler, person who combs flax so as to separate the long line from the short tow fibres after scutching and before spinning
frontage	front part of a burgage plot (qv) nearest the street, on which the dwelling was usually built
indwellers	unprivileged, non-burgess dwellers in a town
Iron Age	the final prehistoric period in Britain named because of the introduction of iron working. Lasted from c 500 BC to AD 400 in Scotland, although the latter half is often termed the Roman Iron Age
lint	flax, which when woven is linen
lint mill	scutch mill in which the flax plant is broken before spinning
lintseed	seed of flax plant. Normally linseed
lister	dyer
listed building	building of special architectural or historic interest, under the terms of the Planning (Listed Buildings and Conservation Areas) (Scotland) Act 1997
mark, merk	13s 4d, two-thirds of £ Scots

midden	refuse heap near a dwelling
motte and bailey	a castle type introduced by the Normans, comprising a timber keep constructed on a large earthen mound with a lower, less well defended enclosure (the bailey) at its base which contained ancillary buildings
Neolithic	meaning 'New Stone Age' and in Scotland representing the period of human settlement between *c* 4000 and 2000 BC
palisade	a timber fence used as a defensive barrier; could also be termed a stockade
Picts	the tribe occupying northern Scotland at the time of the Roman invasion and after
plot	see burgage plot
post-medieval	the period from the sixteenth to the eighteenth century
prehistory	the period of human history before the advent of writing
powerloom	a weaving loom worked by mechanical power
rig	another name for a burgage plot (*qv*)
Samian pottery	shiny red pottery often highly decorated and found throughout the Roman Empire
sasine	an instrument of sasine is the legal document which records the infeftment and transfer of ownership of land or a building
Scheduled	a Scheduled Ancient Monument is protected under the terms of the Ancient Monuments and Archaeological Areas Act 1979
short cists	graves lined with stone slabs and containing a crouched body, dating to the Bronze Age (*qv*)
tolbooth	the most important secular building which served as a meeting place of the burgh council, a place for the collection of market tolls, and often housed the town jail
tolls	payment for use of a burgh market, road or bridge
trial trenching	the archaeological excavation of small trenches to establish whether any remains survive, often part of an evaluation (*qv*)
walker	fuller, person who works a fulling mill that thickens woollen cloth, a process originally done by walking/waulking the cloth (hence waulk song)
watching brief	the archaeological monitoring of excavation works conducted by others

Bibliography

Manuscript sources

East Dunbartonshire Information and Archives, Kirkintilloch
Barony of Kirkintilloch Records
BL/1/1 Burgesses Minutes, 1772–1966
BL/2/1 Town Council Minutes, 1804–20
BL/3/1 Treasurer's Accounts, 1809–1908
BL/3/1b–3 Treasurer Receipt Books, 1615–1772
BL/4/2 Burgh Court Book, 1729–98
Papers found in Westermains, Kirkintilloch
GD85/1 Legal Papers, 1528–1911

National Archives of Scotland, Edinburgh

Stirling Burgh Records	B66/25/498	Royal charters to the burgh and related documents
Forfeited Estates Papers		
1715, Kilsyth	E640/25	Miscellaneous Papers
Gifts and Deposits	GD45/1/215	Dalhousie Muniments

National Library of Scotland, Edinburgh
Mf 85–88(6) *Kirkintilloch Herald*, 1883–1956

National Monuments Record of Scotland, Edinburgh
NMRS Record No. NS67SW 8
NMRS Record No. NS67SW 24
NMRS Record No. NS67SW 27
NMRS Record No. NS67SE 12
NMRS Record No. NS67SE 42
NMRS Record No. NS67SE 46
NMRS Record No. NS67SE 68
NMRS Record No. NS67SE 70
NMRS Record No. NS67SE 71

Printed primary sources

Accounts of the Lord High Treasurer of Scotland, 13 vols, T Dickson *et al* (eds)
    (Edinburgh, 1877–)
Acts of the Lords of Council in Civil Causes, 3 vols, T Thomson *et al* (eds) (Edinburgh,
    1839–)
*Acts of the Lords of Council in Public Affairs, 1501–54: Selections from Acta Dominorum
    Concilii*, R K Hannay (ed) (Edinburgh, 1932)

Acts of the Parliaments of Scotland, 12 vols, T Thomson *et al* (eds) (Edinburgh, 1814–75)

Anderson, A O (ed), *Early Sources of Scottish History, 500–1286* (Edinburgh, 1922)

Balfour Paul, J (ed), *The Scots Peerage*, 9 vols (Edinburgh, 1904–14)

Bower, W, *Scotichronicon*, 8 vols, D E R Watt (ed) (Aberdeen, 1987–93)

Calendar of Documents Relating to Scotland, 5 vols, J Bain *et al* (ed) (Edinburgh, 1881–1986)

Calendar of the State Papers Relating to Scotland and Mary, Queen of Scots, 13 vols, W K Boyd *et al* (eds) (Edinburgh, 1898–1969)

Commissariot Record of Glasgow: Register of Testaments, 1547–1800, F J Grant (ed) (SRS, 1901)

The Court Book of the Burgh of Kirkintilloch 1658–1694, G S Pryde (ed) (SHS, 1963)

Cowan, I B and Easson, D E, *Medieval Religious Houses: Scotland* (London, 2nd edn, 1976)

Cowan, I B (ed), *Parishes of Medieval Scotland* (SRS, 1967)

Defoe, D, *A Tour Through the Whole Island of Great Britain*, P N Furbank and W R Owens (eds) (New Haven, 1991)

Donaldson, G (ed), *The Thirds of Benefices, 1561–72* (SHS, 1949)

Exchequer Rolls of Scotland, 23 vols, J. Stuart *et al* (eds) (Edinburgh, 1878–1908)

Extracts from the Records of the Burgh of Edinburgh, 12 vols, J D Marwick *et al* (eds) (SBRS, 1869–1967)

Extracts from the Records of the Burgh of Glasgow, 11 vols, J D Marwick *et al* (eds) (SBRS, 1876–1916)

Extracts from the Records of the Convention of Royal Burghs of Scotland, 7 vols, J D Marwick (ed) (Edinburgh, 1870–1918)

Fasti Ecclesiae Scoticanae, 10 vols, H Scott *et al* (ed) (Edinburgh, 1915–81)

Firth, C H (ed), *Scotland and the Commonwealth* (SHS, 1895)

Firth, C H (ed), *Scotland and the Protectorate* (SHS, 1899)

Fletcher, J, 'The burgh and parish of Kirkintilloch', in M S Dilke and A A Templeton (eds), *The Third Statistical Account. Vol. vi, The County of Dumbarton* (Glasgow, 1959)

Fullarton, A, *The Topographical, Statistical, and Historical Gazetteer of Scotland* (Glasgow, 1842)

Groome, F H, *Ordnance Gazetteer of Scotland: A Survey of Scottish Topography, Statistical, Biographical, and Historical* (Edinburgh, 1883)

Hamilton Papers, 2 vols, J Bain (ed) (Edinburgh, 1890)

Handyside, R, 'Report on the Burgh of Barony of Kirkintilloch', *Reports of Commissioners on Municipal Corporations, Scotland* (London, 1836)

Heron, R, *Scotland Delineated* (Edinburgh, 1799)

Historie of Scotland wrytten in Latin by Jhone Leslie and translated by James Dalrymple, 3 vols, E G Cody (ed) (Scottish Text Society, 1885–90)

Horsley, J, *Britannia Romana of the Roman Antiquities of Britain* (London, 1732)

Hume Brown, P (ed), *Early Travellers in Scotland* (Edinburgh, 1891)

Hume Brown, P (ed), *Scotland before 1700 from Contemporary Documents* (Edinburgh, 1893)

Hume Brown, P (ed), *Tours in Scotland, 1671 and 1681, by Thomas Kirk and Ralph Thoresby* (Edinburgh, 1892)

Innes, C, *Origines Parochiales*, 2 vols (Edinburgh, 1851–54)

Kirk, J (ed), *The Book of Assumption of the Thirds of Benefices: Scottish Ecclesiastical Rentals at the Reformation* (Oxford, 1995)

Lawrie, A (ed), *Early Scottish Charters, prior to 1153* (Glasgow, 1905)

Lawson, J P, *An Enlarged Gazetteer of Scotland* (Edinburgh, 1841)

Loch, D, *A Tour through most of the Trading Towns and Villages of Scotland; containing notes and observations concerning the Trade, Manufactures, Improvements, &c. of these towns and villages*, 3 vols (Edinburgh, 1778)

MacFarlane, W, *Geographical Collections Relating to Scotland*, 3 vols, A Mitchell (ed) (SHS, 1906–08)

New Statistical Account of Scotland, 14 vols (Edinburgh, 1845)

Pococke, R, *Tours in Scotland: 1747, 1750, 1760*, D W Kemp (ed) (SHS, 1887)

Pryde, G S (ed), *The Burghs of Scotland: A Critical List* (Oxford, 1965)

Pryde, G S, 'Two Burgh Charters, Kirkintilloch, 1211–1214, and Rothesay 1401', *Scottish Historical Review*, xxix (1950)

Regesta Regum Scottorum, 6 vols, G W S Barrow *et al* (eds) (Edinburgh, 1960–)

Register of the Great Seal of Scotland, 11 vols, J M Thomson *et al* (eds) (Edinburgh, 1882–1914)

Register of the Privy Council of Scotland, J H Burton *et al* (eds): First Series, 14 vols (Edinburgh, 1877–98); Second Series, 8 vols (Edinburgh, 1899–1908); Third Series, 16 vols (Edinburgh, 1908–70)

Register of the Privy Seal of Scotland, 8 vols, M Livingstone *et al* (eds) (Edinburgh, 1908–)

Rotuli Scotiae in Turri Londinensi et in Domo Capitulari Westmonasteriensi Asservati, 2 vols, D Macpherson *et al* (ed) (1814–19)

Roy, W, *The Military Antiquities of the Romans in Northern Britain* (London, 1793)

Scottish Population Statistics, including Webster's Analysis of Population, 1755, J G Kyd (ed) (SHS, 1952)

Spottiswoode, J, *History of the Church of Scotland*, 3 vols (Edinburgh, 1845–51)

Statistical Account of Scotland, 1791–99, J Sinclair (ed). New Edition, I R Grant and D J Withrington (eds) (Wakefield, 1978)

Stevenson, J (ed), *Documents Illustrative of the History of Scotland 1286–1306* (Edinburgh, 1870)

Watt, D E R, *Fasti Ecclesiae Scoticanae Medii Aevi ad Annum 1638* (SRS, 1969)

Wilson, J M (ed), *The Imperial Gazetteer of Scotland* (Edinburgh, nd)

Printed books, articles and theses

Adams, I H, *The Making of Urban Scotland* (London, 1978)

Anderson, M O, *Kings and Kingship in Early Scotland* (Edinburgh, 1973)

Atkinson, J A, 'The Manse, Hillhead Road', *DES* (Edinburgh, 1994)

Barclay, G J, 'The Neolithic', in K J Edwards and I B M Ralston (eds), *Scotland after the Ice Age* (Edinburgh, 1997)

Barclay, G J, *Farmers, Temples and Tombs: Scotland in the Neolithic and Early Bronze Age* (Edinburgh, 1998)

Barrow, G W S, *Feudal Britain, The Completion of the Medieval Kingdoms, 1066–1314* (London, 1956)

Barrow, G W S, *Robert Bruce and the Community of the Realm of Scotland* (Edinburgh, 3rd edn, 1988)

Boardman, S, *The Early Stewart Kings: Robert II and Robert III, 1371–1406* (East Linton, 1996)

Bowman, A I, *Kirkintilloch Shipbuilding* (SDLM, 1983)

Breeze, D J, *The Northern Frontier of Roman Britain* (London, 1982)

Breeze, D J, 'The Romans in Stirling and Central Scotland', in J Gifford and F A Walker, *The Buildings of Scotland: Stirling and Central Scotland* (London, 2002)

Brooke, D, *Wild Men and Holy Places: St Ninian, Whithorn and the Medieval Realm of Galloway* (Edinburgh, 1995)

Brown, M, *James I* (Edinburgh, 1994)

Cameron, I B and Stephenson, D, *The Midland Valley of Scotland* (London, 1985)

Campbell, R H, *Scotland since 1707* (Oxford, 1971)

Coppock, J T, *An Agricultural Atlas of Scotland* (Edinburgh, 1976)

Dalrymple Duncan, T, 'Antiquities', in J Horne (ed), *Kirkintilloch*

Dalrymple Duncan, T, 'The house of Comyn', in J Horne (ed), *Kirkintilloch*

Dalrymple Duncan, T, 'The house of Fleming', in J Horne (ed), *Kirkintilloch*

Darton, M, *The Dictionary of Place Names in Scotland* (Orpington, 1994)

Donaldson, G, *Scotland: James V to James VII* (Edinburgh, 1965)

Dunbar, J G, *The Historic Architecture of Scotland* (London, 1966)

Duncan, A A M, *Scotland: the Making of the Kingdom* (Edinburgh, 1975)

Durie, A J, *The Scottish Linen Industry in the Eighteenth Century* (Edinburgh, 1979)

Feachem, R, *Guide to Prehistoric Scotland* (London, 1977)

Ferguson, W, *Scotland: 1689 to the Present* (Edinburgh, 1968)

Finlayson, B and Edwards, K J, 'The Mesolithic', in K J Edwards and I B M Ralston (eds), *Scotland after the Ice Age* (Edinburgh, 1997)

Fisher, I, 'The Early Christian Period in Stirling and Central Scotland', in J Gifford and F A Walker (2002)

Fletcher, J, 'Two Kirkintilloch Antiquities: carved dragon head and short cist', *PSAS*, lxxxvi (1951–52)

Gifford, J and Walker, F A, *The Buildings of Scotland: Stirling and Central Scotland* (London, 2002)

Gordon, G and Dicks, B (eds), *Scottish Urban History* (Aberdeen, 1983)

Grant, A and Stringer, K J, *Medieval Scotland: Crown, Lordship and Community* (Edinburgh, 1993)

Grant, A, *Independence and Nationhood: Scotland 1306–1469* (London, 1984)

Hill, P, *Whithorn and St Ninian: the Excavation of a Monastic Town 1984–91* (Stroud, 1997)

Hillis, J, *Life in a Scottish Country Town in the Victorian Era. Personal Reminiscences: Kirkintilloch, Lenzie, Auchinloch* (Kirkintilloch, 1940)

Holdsworth, P, 'Kirkintilloch: Cowgate', *DES* (Edinburgh, 1986)

Horne, J (ed), *Kirkintilloch* (Kirkintilloch, 1910, reprinted 1993)

Horne, J. 'General expansion', in J Horne (ed), *Kirkintilloch*

Hume, J R, *The Industrial Archaeology of Scotland, 1: The Lowlands and Borders* (London, 1976)

Irvine, J, *The Book of Dumbartonshire*, 2 vols (Edinburgh, 1879)

Johnston, T, *Old Kirkintilloch* (Kirkintilloch, 1937)

Johnston's Gazetteer of Scotland, revised by R W Munro (London, 3rd edn, 1973)

Keppie, L J F, Bailey, G B, Dunwell, A J, McBrien, J H and Speller, K, 'Some excavations on the line of the Antonine Wall 1985–93' *PSAS*, cxxv (1995)

Kirkintilloch WEA Retirement Class, *Two Communities: Springburn and Kirkintilloch: a Chronicle of Glasgow Overspill* (SDLM, 1983)

Lenman, B, *Integration, Enlightenment and Industrialization* (London, 1981)

Lenman, B, *The Jacobite Risings in Britain 1689–1746* (London, 1980)

Lynch, M (ed), *The Early Modern Town in Scotland* (London, 1987)

Lynch, M, 'Urban society, 1500–1700', in R A Houston and I D Whyte (eds), *Scottish Society, 1500–1800* (Cambridge, 1989)

Lynch, M, *Scotland: a New History* (London, 2nd edn, 1992)

Lynch, M, Spearman, M and Stell, G (eds), *The Scottish Medieval Town* (Edinburgh, 1988)

MacDonald, G, 'Further discoveries on the line of the Antonine Wall', *PSAS*, lix (1924–25)

MacDonald, G, *The Roman Wall in Scotland* (Oxford, 1934)

MacGibbon, D and Ross, T, *The Castellated and Domestic Architecture of Scotland from the Twelfth to the Eighteenth Century*, 5 vols (Edinburgh, 1887–92)

Mair, C, *Mercat Cross and Tolbooth* (Edinburgh, 1988)

Martin, D, *Kirkintilloch in Old Picture Postcards* (Zaltbommel, 1985)

Martin, D, *The Forth and Clyde Canal: A Kirkintilloch View* (SDLM, 2nd edn, 1985)

Martin, D, *The Story of Kirkintilloch* (SDLM, 1987)

Martin, D, *The Monkland and Kirkintilloch and Associated Railways* (SDLM, 1995)

Martin, D, *The Comyns at Kirkintilloch* (East Dunbartonshire Archives, 2003)

Martin, D, *Kirkintilloch Castle* (East Dunbartonshire Archives, 2003)

Martin, J, 'Industrial advancement', in J Horne (ed), *Kirkintilloch*

Masser, P and MacSween, A, 'Early Bronze Age Pits at Inchbelle Farm, Kirkintilloch, East Dunbartonshire', *Scottish Archaeological Journal*, xxiv, part i (2002)

Maxwell, G S, *The Romans in Scotland* (Edinburgh, 1989)

Murray, D, *Early Burgh Organisation in Scotland. Vol II, Rutherglen, Lanark, Prestwick, Newton-upon-Ayr, Ayr* (Glasgow, 1932)

Nicholson, R, *Scotland: the Later Middle Ages* (Edinburgh, 1989)

Nicolaisen, W H F, *Scottish Place Names* (London, 1976)

Patrick, D, 'Burghal development', in J Horne (ed), *Kirkintilloch*

RCAHMS, Stilingshire (Edinburgh, 1963)

RCAHMS, *Tolbooths and Town-houses: Civic Architecture in Scotland to 1833* (Edinburgh, 1996)

Ritchie, J N G, 'Prehistoric and Early Historic Stirling and Central Scotland', in J Gifford and F A Walker, *The Buildings of Scotland: Stirling and Central Scotland* (London, 2002)

Ritchie, J N G and Ritchie, A, *Scotland: Archaeology and Early History* (Edinburgh, 1991)

Robertson, A S and revised by Keppie, L, *The Antonine Wall: A Handbook to the Surviving Remains* (Glasgow, 2001)

Robertson, A S, 'Miscellanea Roman-Caledonica', *PSAS*, xcvii (1963–64)

Selwyn, S and Martin, D, *Kirkintilloch: Life and Times* (SDLM, 1994)

Shanks, J, *The Development of Public Services in Kirkintilloch 1870–1914* (Glasgow, 1980)

Skene, W F, *Celtic Scotland*, 3 vols (Edinburgh, 1886)

Speller, K, 'St Flannan's Church, Antonine Wall', *DES* (Edinburgh, 1995)

Stevenson, R D, *Kirkintilloch: Trial Trenching 1978–79* (Glasgow Archaeological Society Bulletin, New Series, No. 9, Spring 1980)

Stewart, A, 'Schools and schoolmasters', in J Horne (ed), *Kirkintilloch*

Strathkelvin District Libraries, *A Walk Through Kirkintilloch's Past* (SDLM, 1982)

Sunter, W, 'Ecclesiastical history', in J Horne (ed), *Kirkintilloch*

The Burgh of Kirkintilloch: the Official Guide (London, nd)

Walker, F A, *The Buildings of Scotland: Stirling and Central Scotland* (London, 2002)

Watson, F J, *Under the Hammer: Edward I and Scotland, 1286–1306* (East Linton, 1998)

Watson, T, *Kirkintilloch, Town and Parish* (Glasgow, 1894)

Watson, W J, *History of the Celtic Place-names of Scotland* (Edinburgh, 1926)

Weir, D, *Kirkintilloch as it Existed Fifty Years Ago* (Glasgow, 1887)

Unpublished reports

Blair, A H and Hastie, M, 'Kelvin Valley Sewer Stage 2 Phase 1 Archaeological Data Structure Report' (unpublished Headland Archaeology client report, 2000)

Casebow, L, 'Excavations at Salford Place, Kirkintilloch 1987–88: Interim Report' (unpublished SUAT archive report)

Stevenson, R D, 'Interim Report on Archaeological Excavations in Kirkintilloch, 1978–79' (unpublished archive report)

Swan, D and James H, 'Peel Park, Kirkintilloch' (unpublished GUARD client report, 2003)

Cartographic sources

Bleau, J, 'The Province of Lennox' (1654). NLS, WD3B/28

Gordon, R and Gordon, J, 'Sterlinshyr and Lennox' (c 1636–52). NLS, Adv. MS.70.2.10 (Gordon 50)

Moll, H, 'Shire of Lenox [i.e. Lennox] or Dunbarton' (1745). NLS, EMS.b.2.1(18)

Ordnance Survey, 1st edition, 1864–65. 1:10560. *Dumbartonshire*, sheet xxv

Ordnance Survey, 1st edition, 1866. 1:500. *Kirkintilloch Town Plan*, Dumbartonshire, sheet xxiv.8.15, xxiv 8.19, xxiv 8.20, xxiv 8.25

Ordnance Survey, 2nd edition, 1899. 1:10560. *Dumbartonshire* sheet 33 NW

Ross, C, 'A map of the shire of Dumbarton' (1777). NLS, EMS.s.182

Roy, W, 'Military Survey of Scotland' (1747–55)

Index

NB: numbers in **bold** refer to figures

Cowgate 18, 19, 22, **24**, 41, 45, **62**, 65–6, 68
   archeological potential 74–5
Cowgate Industrial School 43
Cowgate Subscription School 43
craftsmen 29–30, 38
Craig, John, wright 26
Crawford, Samuel 37
The Cross 17, 19, 20, 22, 47, 61, 70
Cumbernauld 16, 20

Dark Ages 9–10
distillery 64
dockyards 5, 37, 66, 74
drainage 43, 45
Drumteblay 17
Dunbartonshire / Dumbartonshire 2
Duntiblae 64

Eagle Inn (Queen Hotel) 35
East High Street 61
Eastside 7, 19, 22, **27**, 29, 31, 32, 38, 43, 45, 60–5
   archeological potential 74
economy of Kirkintilloch 4–5
   see also industry
Edinburgh and Glasgow Railway 38
electronics industry 5

fairs 28, 40
farming 3, 8, 30
flax steeping 29
Fleming, Sir David 17
Fleming, Malcolm 16
Fleming, Malcolm, Lord 15, 16–17
Fleming, Robert 16
Fleming, Sir Robert, of Biggar 15
Fleming, Thomas 16
Fleming, Rev William 20
Forbes, Sir Arthur 28
Forth and Clyde Canal 4, 5, 7, 34–7, 46, 66
Forth and Clyde Chemical Company 38
Freeland Place 32
Freeland Place School 43
Fyfe, Malcolm **24**

gasworks 44, 64, 68
geology 3
Glasgow Bridge 66
Glasgow Council 26, 28
Glasgow overspill project 46
Glasgow Road 34, **35**, 65
Grey, – , of Duntiblae 32
Guidding, John 18

harbour 34–5, 66
Harestanes 10
Hay, J and J 37, 46, 66
Hay, William 37
Henderson, Robert, mason 26
henges 8
Henrie, Elizabeth and William 18
High Street 7, 17, 18, 19, 22, **23**, 45, 60–5, **62**, **64**
   archeological potential 70, 74
Hillhead 10, 32, 34, 43, 66
Hillhead basin 4, 66
Hillhead Road 47
Holy Family and St Ninian's Roman Catholic Church 43, 60
houses / housing
   17th and 18th century 22, **23**
   19th century 38, 45
   20th century 46–7
   above handloom shops 76, **76**
Hudson, Robert **39**
Hudson Fountain 38, **39**, 60

Inchbelle Farm 8
Inchbelly 2
Inchbelly Bridge 25, 26
industrial estates 46
Industrial School 43
Industrial Society School 43
industry 4–5, 37–40, 46, 66, 68
inns / innkeepers 30, 40, 61
iron, transport 36
iron foundries 5, 37–8, 46, 66, 68

Jacobite risings 28
James IV, king of Scots 17
John Street School 43

Perry Bandstand 38, 60

place names

    Auld (Old) Isle 2

    Dunbartonshire/Dumbartonshire 2

    Inchbelly 2

    Kirkintilloch 3, 9, 13

plots (land) 60, 61

police 43–4

poorhouse 40, 75, **75**

port 34–5, 66

Post Office, Old 22, **24**

prehistoric period 8, 12

    later 13

Pugin and Pugin, architects 43

purls 31

quarries 38

Queen Hotel (Eagle Inn) 35

railways 36, 38, 46

Regent Street 61

rigs (plots) 60, 61

roads 25–6, 28, 34, 45, 65–6

    relief 47, 56, 74

    Roman 9

Robert I, king of Scots 16

Robert II, king of Scots 16

Robertson, William 29

Robertsoune, Margaret 29

Roman camp, Westermains 7

Roman fort 7, 9, 12, 56, **58**, 70

Roman period 7, 8–9, 12–13

Rood House 17

Saddler's Brae 38

St Andrew's Free Church 41, 43

St Columba's Church 43

St David's Church 41, 43

St David's Free Church 43

St Mary's Church

    new 41

    old *see* Auld Kirk

St Ninian 9–10

St Ninian's Church 9, 14, 17, 64

    see also Auld Aisle

Salvation Army Hall 43

sanitation 44–5

schools 22, 41, 43, 60

Sergeant Begbie's school 43

shipyards 5, 37, 66, 74

shops 40

Slimon's Mill **33**, 34, 46

Solsgirth 38

sources of information 6–7

South Bank Iron Works (Star Foundry)

    37–8, 46, 68

Southbank Road 34, 36, 37, 38, 40, 75

Spade Forge Mill 64

spinning 31

Star Foundry (South Bank Iron Works)

    37–8, 46, 68

Stark, Johnne 25

Steeple School 41, 43

Steven, John, merchant 28

Stewart, Matthew 17

Stirling, Sir John 31

street lighting 44

Subscription School, Waterside 43, 64

tailors 29

Temperance Hall 41

textile production 4, 29, 30–4

tolbooth 20, 22, 65

tollbars 45

tollhouse 34, **35**, 65

town council 43–4, 45

Town Hall 3, 41

Town-house *see* Barony Chambers

Townhead 18, 19, 22, **24**, 29, 32, 41, 45,

    47, **62**, 66, **67**, 68, 76

    archeological potential 74

    schools 43

Townhead Bridge 35, 47

trade 28–9

trade routes 25–6, 28

tradesmen 29–30, 38

transport 34–7, 46

Union Street 32, **32**, 41, 43

    excavations **58**, 61